# Confident Humility

# CONFIDENT HUMILITY

*Becoming Your Full Self without Becoming Full of Yourself*

DAN KENT

**Fortress Press**

**Minneapolis**

*To my friend and mentor*
*Paul Eddy,*
*the best teacher I have known*
*and a steadfast model of confident humility*

# CONTENTS

# ACKNOWLEDGMENTS

Right after Barbara said she'd marry me I began handing her drafts of this book. This poor woman has read through this book, including many shoddy drafts, probably twenty times, and she never once refused, complained, or even scoffed. She threw herself into it, doing whatever she could to help make it the best it could be. Thank you, Barbara, for your selfless service to this project.

I graduated from high school with a D average. Thank you to my good friend Randy Barnhart for helping me become a darn good student and for sharpening my mind with all those thrilling, hilarious, nonstop, around-the-clock discussions and debates.

Thank you to my friend and mentor Paul Eddy for your constant encouragement and for letting me teach this content in your theology classes.

Without the ministry of Greg Boyd over the past few decades, this book would never be. And without Shelley, Greg would never be able to do the ministry he has done. Thank you, Greg and Shelley.

If you think this book reads well, it's due in large part to Tony Jones. Places where it reads poorly, well, sometimes

I can be stubborn. Thank you, Tony, for your meticulous editorial feedback.

Thank you, Janice Rohling, Mary Van Sickle, Mary Anderson, Becky Cote, and Rob Kistler at Woodland Hills Church, for allowing me to teach classes on this material as I developed the book. Thank you to Kelly, Juston, and Jordan Eddy for reading an early draft of this book on your road trip to Florida and filling my heart with encouragement.

I had been kicking around the idea for this book for more than ten years when Joe Rueter threatened to beat me up if I didn't actually start writing it.[1] That was just the motivation I needed to get my butt in gear.

Thank you to Di Kistler, Marcus Johannes, Peter Herzog, and Jes Brooks for reading early drafts of the book. And, for all of your encouragement, thank you: Jeremy Berg, Ben Damman, Jonathan Green, Casey Allen, Brandon Andress, Justin Scoggins, Brianna Millet, Dave Barton, Steve Crane, Demetrius Goines Jr., Natalie Frisk, Jacquie Irish, Shelley Boyd, Dan Crandall, Debbie Erstad Donnelly, T. C. Moore, Joshua Burkett, Kurt Willems, Darrell Rohling, Michael Kukuska, Jordan Sutton, Sarah Morgan, Greg and Laurie Gray, Bob and Vicki Barnhart, and Bert and Terri Loveland.

The drawing of Ernst and Freemont was done by the abundantly talented Steve Robbins.

# FOREWORD

I'll start by laying all my cards on the table.

When Dan first asked me to read *Confident Humility* and to consider writing the foreword to it, I wasn't exactly excited. I agreed to do it because Dan has been a close friend for twenty-some years and is the brainchild and host of my podcast (*Greg Boyd: Apologies & Explanations*). Also, knowing Dan as I do, I knew he wouldn't bother to write a book if he didn't have something important to say that wasn't already being said.

But *humility*? What important and new thing could anyone possibly have to say about *that*?

I could not have been more wrong! To say that this well-written, witty, and brilliantly argued book has something important and new to say about humility feels like a significant understatement. In the spirit of Dallas Willard, Dan addresses one of the most persistent problems that Christians face. Why does our faith in God's transforming love transform us so little? Or better, is there a way of thinking about God's love that will better open us up to experience more of its transforming power?

*Confident Humility* makes a compelling case that there is.

Just as a teaser, consider this. Christians have traditionally assumed people are inherently bad and have thus held that people generally esteem themselves too highly. In this view, people need to humble themselves by cultivating a lower estimation of themselves. By contrast, the modern self-esteem movement has assumed that people are inherently good and generally esteem themselves too lowly. In this view, people need to be given greater confidence in their inherent worth and abilities.

Pulling together insights from Scripture, psychology, and theology, Dan argues forcefully that neither of these models is consistent with Jesus's teaching, neither is internally consistent, and neither succeeds in helping people.

In their place, Dan asks, What if we stopped focusing on how we esteem ourselves and instead focus on how God esteems us, as is revealed especially by Jesus's sacrificial death on the cross? Dan demonstrates that when people's worth is grounded in the objective reality of God's love, it frees them from the need to engage in the futile mental game of trying to cultivate a lower or higher self-esteem. Rather, with their core sense of worth settled, people are free to simply see themselves as they actually are and to therefore openly acknowledge, and continue to work on, areas in which they are still weak or wounded.

Read this book carefully and apply its teachings to your life and I believe you'll find yourself getting set free from the overly incriminating and/or overly congratulatory voices in your head. And this, in turn, will free you to be more profoundly transformed by God's perfect love for you.

When our confidence is anchored in God's love, in other words, we are free to become our full self without becoming full of ourselves.

Gregory A. Boyd

# CHAPTER 1.

# A TALE OF TWO DITCHES

Mom and I were not religious when I was a boy. In fact, our first church experience was downright embarrassing. Somewhere in the middle of the preacher's passionate sermon, Mom stood up and shouted, "That's a bunch of bullshit!" The next thing I knew Mom had my wrist and was dragging me out of the pew before the wide eyes and dropped jaws of a thousand congregants. She wasn't trying to cause a scene or be disrespectful. The preacher simply told a story from the Bible that upset her, and she reacted. To understand why, you have to understand a little about my mom.

Mom was young when she had me. Raised by a family thick with dysfunction on a failing farm near a small town in nowhere Minnesota, she grew up a lonely and insecure girl. So when an older man showered her with attention, and with what she believed was love, she was unprepared to protect herself from him. She fell for his predatory behaviors and became pregnant with me when she was only thirteen.

She was a tough girl, though. Family Services pressured her to have an abortion, but she refused. Because of her small size, giving birth meant having her abdomen cut open. She endured that. Being pregnant at only thirteen amplified the judgmental imaginations of the town and triggered cruel teasing from her fellow seventh-graders. She endured that, too. She even agreed to marry my dad when their families decided marriage would look best. They found a church in South Dakota willing to perform the marriage, and, after a brief drive, she became a wife to a man almost twice her age.

Dad made impressive personal changes at some point in his life and did some good things for himself and for others. But back then, when Mom was married to him, he was not well. He was abusive, controlling, and dangerous. The danger peaked one summer when Dad bought an old farmhouse with no running water or insulation at the end of a long dirt road surrounded by miles of nothing but corn fields and marsh. Mom refused to live in such isolation with him, so she escaped with me and we fled to Minneapolis, away from Dad, away from the small town, and away from her troubled family.

What Mom did still inspires me. You should've seen her. She battled monsters that would immobilize almost anyone else. Mom was too young to vote or buy cigarettes, but there she was—without even a junior-high education—responsible for herself and her bright-eyed toddler, alone in a big city. She took terrible jobs, worked long hours, and never accepted public assistance. Mom had to do twice the parental work of a married couple with a fraction of the maturity and preparation. Yet she found a way to lift us to a place where we might grow into healthy and good people.

You can imagine how challenging this was for her. Grandma tried to help. A regular watcher of TV evangelists, Grandma thought the answer to our problems was God and church. While I ultimately think she was right, this particular church on that particular Sunday was not helpful. On that day the preacher told the story of how Lot's daughters made their father drunk so they could have sex with him (Genesis 19:30–38). My teenage mom, burdened with so much toil and pierced with so much emotional pain from sexual perversion and boundary violation, couldn't listen anymore.

## A SCIENTIST AND A SOCIOPATH

I found church again as a teenager. Unlike Mom's experience, church liberated me. To understand why, you have to understand what it was like growing up as I did.

In some ways, Mom and I grew up together. When I was a kid, so was she. Strangers were gobsmacked to learn I was her son. "I thought you were brother and sister," they'd say.

In many other ways we grew up apart. Pregnancy and a traumatic marriage interrupted Mom's development. I remember her having a nagging sense she needed to catch up on what she'd missed in life. Her desire for normalcy swept her up in a chase for a husband, and a father for me—to maybe have a normal family. She wanted a job and longed for friends, like normal people. This chase led her to many lousy boyfriends (and a couple good ones), toilsome jobs, and alcoholism. She worked long hours to buy as much normalcy as she could. And when she wasn't working, she was often pursuing romance and social vitality. She wasn't intentionally neglectful—I can't imagine a mom who cared more for a son—but she was ambitious, which led to time-consuming distractions. In many ways, I was left to grow up on my own.

I'll be honest, life overwhelmed me. Growing up like I did, I had to become a social scientist. I'd watch people, trying to understand why they did what they did and how they went about their lives. Kids like me have to figure out big things on our own, like what it means to be a boy, what the point of school is, and what the right way to be is. There are also a million day-to-day things, like how to think about money, how to handle loss and disappointment, how to handle winning, how to tell a good story, what to do when afraid, how to handle boredom, how to be good in conversation, and so much more.[1]

Most kids can absorb cozy defaults from their parents. In any given situation, they can simply go with how Mom or Dad does something. Kids like me must learn everything from scratch. It's confounding. If you could peek in on me back then, you'd see a blond-haired boy, dumbfounded and baffled, staring into numb space, trying to make sense of it all. In elementary school I was even diagnosed with something called *delayed comprehension* (it took me forever to figure out what *that* meant).[2]

Adding to the perplexity, we moved many times. Mom seemed forever in pursuit of better opportunities—better jobs, better neighborhoods, better boyfriends. We lived life always ready to pack up and split.

When you go from school to school like I did, you discover just how fickle social effectiveness can be, and you begin to see just how arbitrary personality is. For instance, there'd be schools where I'd connect easily with popular kids. Then, sometimes only days later, at a new school, popular kids would reject me. It was maddening.[3]

It's hard to develop an effective personality when acceptance seems so illogical. It all seemed random to me.

Thank God for *Fletch*, my favorite movie as a boy. Chevy Chase plays an investigative reporter who accomplishes everything he needs to accomplish by taking on false personas and duping gullible strangers. Fletch would alter his voice, wear wigs or fake teeth, and suddenly be an airplane mechanic, a government official, a religious guru, or whatever else a situation demanded. I admired how he would change himself, and how he knew exactly what bogus things he needed to say to exploit the gullibility of others.

On a smaller level, without the false teeth or funny wigs, I learned to do the same. I discovered just how easy personality was to fake, and I learned how to change it on command. The capriciousness of others and the malleability of personality meant that people can be gamed, and social situations can be manipulated to get approval and validation. I became good at pretending, and flat out lying, to get what I wanted. In other words, I went from being a young social scientist to becoming a young sociopath.

You should've seen me. To the jocks I spoke jock, to the nerds I spoke nerd, to the artists I spoke, well, artistic gibberish. I became the stereotypical chameleon, pulling everybody's strings, playing them all to my favor. Then, having mastered this role of chameleon, I began evolving into the more advanced role of con artist. For instance, in seventh grade I forged a letter to my teacher from my doctor excusing me from class so I could go to the nurse's office to take my "megolipthious pills." In reality, I'd sneak out of school and go to the gas station to buy candy—which I'd then sell to my peers for a profit. I did many things like this. I even stole money—money I didn't need—from good employers just because I enjoyed outsmarting their systems.

These terrible behaviors gave me a sense of control over a reality that seemed otherwise overwhelming and haphazard. They were shortcuts that allowed me to dance around the hard work of developing any real character or competence.

## DISCOVERING THE DITCHES

In junior high I fell in love with comic books. Dave, the owner of the comic-book shop where I'd binge-read comics, happened to volunteer at a church youth group, and he invited me to join him. As a budding sociopath, I felt great pressure to be liked. But at church this pressure was strangely nonexistent. Relative to the harsh social economy of school, acceptance here was easy; nobody had to earn it. Every Wednesday I'd go, play volleyball, and flirt with the girls. I'd also listen to the weekly teachings, and even began attending the Sunday service.

The teachings really appealed to me. They taught me about things like character and about doing the right thing even when it means not getting the outcome I want. They also introduced me to new metrics for success, like being trustworthy and having integrity. The shortcuts I'd taken in life were effective, but I could sense my own shallowness even then. I had very little integrity and had become wholly untrustworthy. I went back to church again and again, and I kept learning until, at some point, I believed.

Well, most of it. I didn't believe all of it. My new church believed with great conviction that everybody—each of us—is completely defective and morally powerless because of sin. Spiritual maturity meant learning to see yourself as God supposedly saw you: a hopelessly broken vessel of sin. This message was not always explicit, but it was always implied. Someone might share in group prayer, "Lord, I am a despicable sinner, hopelessly dependent on you," and others in the group would whisper "amen," or would nod in quiet affirmation.

But I didn't nod, and I couldn't bring myself to affirm such a low view. My reasons were simple, if not simplistic. For one thing, the message didn't cohere with the paintings on the church's walls. I'm sure you've seen these paintings. The ones where movie-star Jesus, with his perfect hair and teeth, carries giddy children on his shoulders. His posture and affect toward these kids, combined with the carefree spirits of those around him, seemed to imply anything but *despicable vessels of sin.*

For another thing, the message didn't align with how those in the church treated me. They didn't treat me like a despicable sinner—and compared to most of them, I actually was! They embraced me and treated me with great dignity. Honestly, those believers changed my life. That church was my first experience of community, one where I felt genuinely important and loved.

Plus, it was the early 1990s and the self-esteem movement was in full force—infiltrating television programs and school curricula, serenading us all with a constant parade of euphoric propaganda. Like others in my generation, I was soaked in the ideology of self-esteem and was resistant to any contrary teachings. Posters, school movies, and class lectures conditioned us daily: "You are a winner," "You are special," "You are good enough just the way you are." Success in life, these positivity police proclaimed, requires high amounts of self-esteem.

In stark contrast to what my church taught, my society taught that I must learn to love myself and believe in myself, and I must fight against feelings of smallness. This left me in a predicament. Church had drawn my attention beyond the level of personality, down to personhood and character. And here, at this deeper level, I found conflicting philosophies. My church told me: "You are bad." My society told me: "You are great."

It's strange to me that, for something so important, there would be these two widely held yet contradicting perspectives. I call them the *Ditch of Smallness* and the *Ditch of Bigness*. They pull on each of us, from childhood to old age, and cause tremendous havoc in our lives.

## THE DITCH OF SMALLNESS: NOBODY DESERVES A TROPHY

Church was my first encounter with the Ditch of Smallness, so I remain most interested in Christian variations of this ditch. But people come to this ditch for many reasons, and from many directions.[4] What they all have in common, no matter how deep in the ditch they travel, is they all contribute to a downward pull. This downward pull emerges from a common passion to defend what they consider the right view of self and a corresponding repulsion to anything that competes with, or muddles, that view of self.

The supposed right view of self is simple. Humans are bad. There's no point seeking out the right psychiatric disorder, human nature *is* the disorder. You'll hear religious folks in this ditch go on and on about things like their finitude, their sinful nature, and the cognitive effects of sin. These people aren't simply complaining, they're diagnosing. They are claiming that each of us has serious spiritual deficiencies that we can do nothing about. In fact, they say, even when we appear to be doing something good, there is always some sinful motive beneath the surface negating all actual goodness. As Luther put it, people "are flesh, they can savor of nothing but the flesh; therefore, 'free-will' can avail only to sin."[5] No matter how good we seem, in reality we are each nothing "but rottenness and a worm."[6]

I know what you're thinking: *not the type of people I'd invite to a party*. But give your brain a few seconds, and it will call forth a flood of anecdotes to support such beliefs. Think of the sadistic stepfather who beats his stepson, the girl raped at the frat party, or the con artist who bilked the old lady across the street out of her retirement money. Heck, every episode of the evening news is a closing argument confirming this apparent depravity of our nature. The more we come to accept this depravity, Team Smallness claims, the closer we come to reality, and the better off we will be.

Pride always denies depravity. Because of this, Team Smallness considers pride Enemy Number One, our nemesis, the supervillain we must work to avoid at all costs. This is not easy since our default tendency is to make grandiose evaluations of ourselves. To fight against this tendency, we must throw ourselves in the opposite direction. We must abnegate, minimize, diminish, and deflate ourselves, keeping our self-appraisals sober and always focused on the negative. We must extinguish the self as much as possible, striving always to become an empty vessel.

I've known many Christians for whom this pursuit of smallness seems almost like a religion within their religion. People dedicate themselves to the ministry of smallness and martyr themselves in a war against all pride. This dedication to downwardness is deemed necessary because grandiose positivity is ever-present, always tugging us upward. Resistance must be constant, effort must be perpetual. Our radars must always be on, probing the depths of our psyche for renegade puffs of self-esteem. "Though I was still confessing pride I knew I wasn't sufficiently convicted of it," confesses Pastor C. J. Mahaney, deep in the throes of his hunt.[7]

As a boy trying to raise myself in the big, bad world, I wanted to have a sense of what my potential was. I'm not even talking about things like vocation, social status, fame, or any measure like that. I'm simply talking about the possibility of having healthy relationships, controlling my emotions, managing my money, maintaining physical health, being a good person, and so forth. But to Team Smallness, what's possible for my life has a simple and sober answer: Nothing good is possible. Whatever I seek for myself, I can't get there.[8] Well, that is, I can't get there, or do anything good, *on my own*. God can still do good things in me. But absent divine intervention, only sin and self-centeredness lie before me.

The heavy gravity and the obsession with self-abnegation in the Ditch of Smallness is tiresome. The endless hunt for pride and the constant scorekeeping of unrighteous behaviors, the victory dance every time a public figure has a fall from grace or gets caught in a sin, or the guy in every class I teach (there's always one) who raises his hand whenever I merely *hint* that people might have personal responsibility to do some good thing or another, who says, "You mean God does it for us, right?" It's exhausting.

Yet, when I read how Jesus lived and acted, I see nothing like how Team Smallness wants me to live and act. Sure, Jesus attacked the arrogant, but he mostly lifted low people up. And rather than degrading people, he worked steadfastly at redeeming their dignity. Jesus had a way of life that was radically contrary to what Team Smallness promotes.

## THE SEDUCTIVE CHARM OF SMALLNESS

To modern ears, the Ditch of Smallness can sound harsh and loathsome. And, in many ways, it is. But to be fair, the ditch can also be comforting and beautiful as it plays out in real life. For one thing, it can be a welcome alternative to the abundant amounts of superficial positivity we endure every day. Marketers, politicians, salespeople, and advocates from the Ditch of Bigness flood the world with hype. But those in the Ditch of Smallness remain mostly immune to it.

I also appreciate the attention Team Smallness gives to sin. The world makes it easy for us to deny our sinfulness, and we each become specialists at deluding ourselves into thinking we are more righteous than we really are. Team Smallness takes sin too seriously for it to be ignored, and there's real value in that.

Perhaps what I appreciate most about Team Smallness is how they treat people who are struggling with a weakness or a failure of any kind. My mother developed an alcohol addiction, and I'd sometimes sit with her at her support groups. People in these groups would share shocking things with one another. One guy stole money from his daughter to buy cocaine. There was a lady who drove drunk with her infant in the back seat and crashed into a busy restaurant. A grandfather told us how he got super drunk before going to his granddaughter's birthday party where he proceeded to urinate in his pants before passing out on the living-room floor. What's eminently endearing about the spirit of Team Smallness is how they respond to such confessions. In Mom's group, confessors were embraced with empathetic affirmations. "We all make mistakes," they'd say, and "you're only human." It was this spirit of acceptance that made it easy for Mom to confess her own struggles without fear of rejection.

When you confess your brokenness to someone in the Ditch of Smallness, you will most likely be embraced and accepted just as you are. This warmth is, in its own way, a charming alternative to our judgmental, standoffish world. Jesus also models radical acceptance, and for this reason the Ditch of Smallness can appear very holy. And when they accept others without judgment, they really *are* being holy.

But motivation matters. The more I've learned about the Ditch of Smallness, the more I've come to see that the acceptance modeled there is an incomplete expression of the acceptance Jesus models. The reason has to do with *what* is being accepted. Since Team Smallness assumes we are all broken, insignificant zeroes—each thoroughly and hopelessly bad—people who confess depravity take on a false sense of authenticity. A person admitting weakness is seen as *being real*, while a person acknowledging a strength or professing even the simplest of spiritual gifts might be looked at with distrust. The depraved, the ineffective, the lowly are, in this distorted way, *esteemed*. The acceptance is conditional. In fact, oftentimes it's not really even the confessor being affirmed, but the confession of powerlessness.

Some Christians I've met have even come to see lowliness as being somehow holy, and the fact that Jesus spent so much time with the lowly reinforces this belief. "Blessed are the poor in spirit," Jesus says, and supposedly hangs out with them because there's something authentic, even desirable, about being poor in spirit.

But this is not the case. It's simply not true. As Dallas Willard observes, "Jesus did not say, 'Blessed are the poor in spirit *because* they are poor in spirit.' He did not think, 'What a fine thing it is to be destitute of every spiritual attainment or quality.'"[9] Jesus hung out with the poor in spirit as a public validation of their worth. He did this in spite of their destitution, not as an affirmation of their destitution. Otherwise he would not have told so many—like the woman caught in adultery (John 8:11)—to change their ways. Jesus affirmed sinners because they are worthy of affirmation. He challenged the false belief that sin makes people less worthy. Team Smallness wants us to put our weaknesses at the center of how we view ourselves. Jesus advocates for the exact opposite. Repent from your weakness, he tells us. This implies that defectiveness is not the essence of who or what we are.

## THE DITCH OF BIGNESS: EVERYONE DESERVES A TROPHY

Believe it or not, the view promoted by Team Smallness was the standard way people saw themselves in America for many decades. But people, it seems, can take only so much smallness before pushing back. Resistance to the Ditch of Smallness in America arose in the last hundred years, evolving into the two-headed monster of the self-esteem movement and the positive-thinking movement, both of which I will explore in depth.

There's a wide variety of ideas in the Ditch of Bigness, but common to all is a constant upward push of our self-assessments, along with a preoccupation with positivity. Just like Team Smallness, Team Bigness wants us to establish the correct view of self and to avoid the incorrect view. But what they consider correct and incorrect is exactly opposite of Team Smallness.

The right view of self is that, deep down, people are fundamentally good. "We are God-breathed and made in the image of God," the religious in this ditch will say. Selfishness, hatred, and destruction are not our natural states. To the contrary, they are symptoms of a *disruption* to our natural state. Carl Rogers, considered the father of humanistic psychology, counseled many troubled patients over his long and celebrated career. Reflecting on these patients, he concluded, "In a great majority of cases [these patients] despise themselves, regard themselves as worthless and unlovable."[10] In other words, people with the most serious woes in their lives seem to be *heroes* of the Ditch of Smallness!

As you travel along in the Ditch of Bigness, you'll hear gurus, therapists, and life coaches flatter you with grandiose assessments of your greatness. You'll be encouraged to trust your intuitions and told that everything you need to be great resides somehow inside of you. They'll try to convince you that the only thing keeping you from a vibrant and healthy life is negativity and a failure to fully understand how great you really are.

If you don't subscribe to this view, you might be thinking: *What land of lollipops and Christmas sweaters are these people living in?!?* But give your brain a moment and it will call forth a dazzling collage of human achievement and human goodness. We are a people who measure the universe, transplant organs, fly to the moon, feed the homeless, and rescue children from burning buildings. Yes, criminals and rapists exist, but so do doctors and teachers. And for every Adolf Hitler and Bernie Madoff there is a Nelson Mandela and a Malala Yousafzai.

If we are fundamentally good, then shame must be a lie, because shame is a feeling of being fundamentally bad. Therefore, shame is our real enemy, not pride.

Watch how all of this plays out in theories of self-development. According to Carl Rogers, we each have powerful resources within us that can fuel the healthy growth of our good and unique selves. Our problem is that we suffocate our true selves as we grow up. We surrender our true selves to please others. In becoming what we think others want us to become, we hand over our rightful authority to them. And in so doing, we inevitably become something we were not meant to be. All of our innate resources will flourish in our lives if we can simply get out of the way and if we can keep others from dictating who we should be, what we should think, and how we should behave. If given the space and authority, our wonderfully unique and empowered true selves will emerge.

Perhaps this sounds wishy-washy or abstract. Watch a toddler at the dinner table and you might see her sabotage her authority in this way. Suppose she desires to slather mashed potatoes on her face but opts not to for fear of angering her parents. The child chooses to be a good girl and not slather the potatoes. She has, in that moment, repressed a piece of herself for others. She has handed over a small amount of her authority. This may seem inconsequential, but it's the kind of habit that can accumulate into an inertia-of-surrender that can supposedly blind the self later on in life. In handing over our authority to others, we become dependent on others in ways we were not meant to be. We usurp ourselves. Our own magnificent systems of evaluation are smothered under layer upon layer of compromise made to please others. We lose touch with who we really are.

Many of the urges I might declare shameful really aren't. Rather, those urges are there for a reason and ought to be given air and light. I must take back authority and begin to trust my true self—my *inner child*—again. Our job, according to Team Bigness, is to seize back authority and to defy all shame. This is not easy. We're surrounded by psychological gravities trying to pull us down. To combat this, we must constantly replenish our mental helium, working diligently to prop up the self, to inflate self-confidence, and to keep ourselves above all self-doubt.

To modern ears, the Ditch of Bigness often sounds wise. But when you look closer, I think you will find it vacuous. The praise is often baseless, and the positivity arbitrary. There was a poster in my middle school with a famous athlete pointing toward the viewer. Written in big letters the poster said: YOU ARE SPECIAL. Even then I remember thinking *how does he know I'm special?* The assumption underlying the poster, of course, is that *everyone* is special. But even as a boy, I understood that everyone can't be special, at least not without wrecking what special means. But that's how Team Bigness operates. They fill the air with these free-floating compliments. There's rarely logic or justification for any of it.

Whereas the Ditch of Smallness browbeats us into

believing we can never get to where we want to go on our own, the Ditch of Bigness cajoles us into believing there *is* no place to go. We're already there. *You are great just the way you are.* It can become almost manic, the obsession with stoking positivity and the animated preoccupation with boosting self-esteem. And it can sound so good. But when I look at Jesus, and when I read the Bible, I find a different message than what Team Bigness promotes. God expects us to change and to evolve into better people. Yes, we are *loved* just as we are. But for that very reason God wants us to become more.

## THE FALSE BEAUTY OF BIGNESS

When you're around Team Bigness you don't have to be embarrassed about your strengths, and I like that. You don't have to pretend that you are dumber or uglier or less competent than you are. In fact, when you're striving to realize the goodness inside of you, as Team Bigness encourages, the more of these good qualities you can highlight, the better.

Also, the idea that I'd be better off loving myself than hating myself seems undeniable. So too, if we were all to love ourselves, it's only natural that we would all be better people. And finally, if we were all better people, society would be better as well. "Many, if not most, of the major problems plaguing society have roots in the low self-esteem of many of the people who make up society," proclaimed Neil Smelser, one of the academic figureheads of the self-esteem movement of the 1980s.[11]

This compelling line of thought swept America off its feet, and self-esteem took on a ferocious life of its own in the late twentieth century. We loved loving ourselves!

The importance of self-esteem became common knowledge. Celebrities raised awareness for it. Coaches coached it. Teachers taught it. The government legislated it.

But self-esteem failed.

It just didn't work. We were all sucked into a giant falsehood, a collective strange dream, that slow-played us into feeling better about ourselves while simultaneously lowering our standards. We heaped positivity onto our children in the hopes of inflating the mythic self-esteem balloon inside them. Americans are now overflowing with self-esteem, scoring toward the top of all self-esteem measures. But this abundance of self-esteem has not been the blessing we hoped it would be.

In 2003, Roy Baumeister and his colleagues found that self-esteem does not improve human effectiveness in any relevant way. Having higher self-esteem does not, for instance, reduce the chances of children smoking, taking drugs, or engaging in early sex. High self-esteem fails to improve the quality or duration of relationships. The embarrassing lack of any measurable advantage of having self-esteem led these researchers to conclude, "We have not found evidence that boosting self-esteem . . . causes benefits."[12] In fact, they found the opposite. Improving self-esteem deteriorates outcomes—it makes things worse! For instance, the higher a person's self-esteem, the more likely they are to experiment with drugs and sex. Rather than improving school performance, more research suggests that increased self-esteem diminishes performance for struggling students. Basically, self-esteem turns us into poor-performing, risk-taking, self-obsessed hedonists. Psychologist Paul Vitz said it well: Boosting self-esteem is "like printing your own money—it leads to a false prosperity."

Some people aren't bothered by such false prosperity. In fact, they consider it beneficial to think of yourself as smart even if you're not. They believe there is power in positive thinking itself.

## POSITIVE THINKING IN THE DITCH OF BIGNESS

It's no coincidence that the positive-thinking movement gained momentum alongside the self-esteem movement. After all, they both emerged in reaction to the same clouds of negativity billowing from the Ditch of Small-ness. In retaliation to the negativity of Team Smallness, the positive-thinking movement fosters positivity. They encourage it, nurture it, surround themselves in it—heck, they'd drink it if they could.

When we see things that make us happy, we feel posi-tive. The positive-thinking movement goes a step further. They strain to see positivity no matter what is actually there to be seen. If we can conjure positivity and main-tain it, they claim, we can establish a positivity inertia that can have almost magical capabilities to improve our lives. Barbara Ehrenreich, in her book on the dangers of positivity, sums up the tactic well, saying, "The trick, if you want to get ahead, is to simulate a positive outlook, no matter how you might actually be feeling."[13] In other words, if you don't have a positive outlook, fake it. If you don't have enthusiasm, pretend that you do—and radiate it!

These positive thinkers consider focusing on the posi-tives as a way to activate powers within that can change not only us but external reality as well. Just watch how some of these positive thinkers act like Jedi masters sum-moning the Force. Self-development guru Wayne Dyer likes to tell his audience, "When you change the way you look at things, the things you look at change."[14] Talk about a superpower!

If positivity is our superpower, then negativity is our kryptonite. When we attend to negative things, or interact with negative people, the entire positivity structure within us can crumble. To keep our positivity power potent, we must work diligently to block out all negativity. This includes avoiding all negative people, avoiding all negative places, and even avoiding the news, as the news often fixates on all that is negative in the world.

For many of these folks, positivity trumps everything—including reason. Joel Osteen declares: "You cannot hang out with negative people and expect to live a positive life." Then, moments later and with the same conviction (I kid you not), he proclaims: "Other people do not determine your potential."[15] This incoherence is the inevitable outcome of the positive-thinking ideology.

True, the Bible encourages us to think about positive things. For instance, Paul tells us, "Whatever is true, whatever is noble, whatever is right, whatever is pure, whatever is lovely, whatever is admirable—if anything is excellent or praiseworthy—think about such things" (Philippians 4:8). But notice the conditional language Paul uses. He tells us *when* to think about positive things. He says, "whatever *is* true," or "*if* anything is excellent," *then* "think about such things." Paul is reminding us that there really are good things—God's creation is amazing!—and that we need to dwell on these things. Paul is preaching gratitude, which is very different from positivity. Gratitude encourages an appreciation for things that are already there but need to be recognized. Positivity is a conjured feeling no matter what is actually there.

In the end, the positivity of Team Bigness is just as vacuous as self-esteem. From motivational posters that claim, "A Positive Attitude Makes a Positive Life," to hospital teddy bears with little T-shirts that read, "Even Cancer Can't Defeat a Positive Attitude," the balloon of positivity is often stuffed with grandiose expectation and hope—which, we will see, it never lives up to.

Pretending to be positive when we are not leads to inauthenticity. The more we pretend to be positive, the more we lose touch with who we really are. This is important. In fact, for many in the Ditch of Bigness, it's a slap in the face. Losing touch with *who we really are* is the major crisis they've been trying to avoid all along—it's what started them on this ridiculous journey to begin with!

|  | Team Smallness | Team Bigness |
|---|---|---|
| **You are** | bad | good |
| **Are you trustworthy?** | no | yes |
| **You avoid** | pride | shame |
| **You dwell on the** | negative | positive |
| **Your goal for yourself is** | deflation | inflation |

## HOPING FOR HIGHER GROUND

As a growing boy looking for light, the loudest voices and the brightest minds I could find left me in darkness. Voices from one ditch chanted, "You are bad!" Voices from the other ditch chanted, "You are great!" One crowd assumed "you can't get there." The other proclaimed "you're already there." What I find curious is that the most salient insights from each ditch happen to be about the flaws of the opposite ditch. Each accuses the other of promoting an unhealthy and skewed view of the self—and they're both right! Each sees profound spiritual insecurity in the other—and again, they're both right! Whenever you find two contraries that are each right about the other being wrong, it can only mean one thing. They're both wrong.

This troubled me because there seemed to be only two options. If they're both wrong, then there's no discernible truth about the self beneath the level of personality. And if there's no meaningful truth beneath the level of personality, then there's no real reason not to be a sociopath—I was better off before I found church! If personality is all there is, then mastering the game of manipulating it to get what I want is the best I can hope for.

But wait. Perhaps we can combine the strengths of each ditch or find a balance between them. This is tempting but not easy to do. In fact, it's impossible. As long as we're operating with the same presuppositions as the ditches, we will always devolve into one ditch or the other. There can be no balance. Once we embrace even a minor tentacle, we get pulled deeper and deeper—into one ditch, away from the other.

Say you find some clever aphorism that intrigues you, like, "Let Go, Let God," or, "Surround Yourself with Positive People." You might even print it on a T-shirt or put it on a poster and think it's cute and no big deal. But as soon as you try to live out the aphorism, or as soon as you start questioning it, you get pulled into deeper places. As you try, for instance, to surround yourself with positive people, you soon get the epiphany to avoid negative people. And it doesn't take much mental power to infer from all these efforts that your primary problem is not you but those around you. And now you are only inches away from encountering the foundation of the Ditch of

Bigness, that you are fundamentally good and it's other people that cause you to stumble.

The reason I call these perspectives ditches is because you can't be in both at the same time, and once you start into either, it's easy to end up at the bottom. And just like ditches, traveling in them is toilsome. The Ditches of Smallness and Bigness both lead us down the same stale spiritual paths. They both cultivate passivity. They both foster powerlessness. They both nourish the soil of oppression. And, as we'll see, they promote shame and arrogance.

Good news! There really is another way, a way that extends before us like a road between these two ditches. An answer exists that secures us, empowers us, and deactivates both shame and pride in our lives, while also making real confidence possible.

The answer is humility.

More specifically, the answer is humility *as Jesus teaches it*. We're surrounded by counterfeits of the humility Jesus teaches, and we must travel with great caution. Imposter concepts of humility are waiting to ambush us from each ditch, eager to draw us into their traps. Instead of empowering us, popular notions of humility often amplify our burdens, adding fuel to the fires of our pathologies.

The humility endorsed here is different. God made us to be empowered and proactive. We were made to be secure, and we have the right to be confident. Humility, as Jesus teaches it, is the surest path to get us there. In fact, it's the only path.

# CHAPTER 2.

# THE ROAD TO SECURITY

In college I took a class on the teachings of Jesus. One day Professor Herzog, moving up and down the rows of desks, gave each student a small piece of paper with a word on it. Whatever word we were given would be the topic of our course paper. As he came closer to my desk, I began hoping for something exciting like atonement or sanctification. You can imagine my disappointment when I unfolded my paper to reveal the least-exciting word of all: humility. I tried to trade my word with someone but had no luck. So, I took a deep breath and resigned myself to my burden.

As was my style, I started my research by reading how other Christian thinkers understood humility. They all—literally all of them—followed the same general line of thought. "In order to define humility," Wayne Mack proposed, "we will start by looking at the definition of humility's opposite: pride."[1] This strategy seemed universal. "We all agree that pride is the opposite of humility," echoed Peter Wagner.[2]

**Pride**

↑
↓

**Humility**

At first, this rang true to me because I couldn't imagine a person being both humble and arrogant at the same time. But then I noticed something curious. These thinkers had bound humility to pride in a teeter-totter sort of way—the more pride you have, the less humility you have, and vice versa. I soon noticed that hitching humility to pride like this seemed to energize downwardness and inevitably led to a race to the bottom. We all want to be humble. But to be humble, according to this definition, we must eliminate pride—and all of its pro-self, grandiose bluster. Our goal must be to mold ourselves in the opposite way: lowly, small, and anti-self.

Once we've accepted humility as the opposite of pride, and once we've decided we want more humility, the pursuit of smallness is unavoidable. There is no other direction to go. As Mack confesses, "in the Christian life, the way up is down."[3] So we hustle to remove all traces of self-praise and self-sufficiency from our lives, we belittle ourselves and smite all positivity. It can become a strange, downward game, where points are scored based on how much esteem we *lose*. Many Christian leaders participate in this contest.

- Humility is to accept "where God is all, self is nothing" (Andrew Murray).[4]
- Humility is to know we are "totally worthless before [God]" and that each of us is "desperately

wicked and incapable of anything worthwhile in God's sight" (Stuart Scott).[5]

- Humility is "a true knowledge and experience of yourself as you are, a wretch, filth, far worse than nothing" (*The Cloud of Unknowing*).[6]

Nietzsche called those who play this game "little-souled," because they become too self-denigrated to recognize their own worth.[7] I call them *humilitants* because of how militantly they pursue anti-pride humility.[8] Humilitants give everything toward becoming nothing. You've seen people one-upping each other. You'll find humilitants one-downing each other as they strive with great fervor toward realizing a more and more insignificant self.

The mindset of a humilitant becomes one of inverted perfectionism. Those trapped here get tangled up in an absurd pursuit: chasing excellence at being devoid of all excellence. Their peculiar passion results in a "bizarre piety," says Greg Boyd, "where people think they're praising God by beating themselves up—*I'm altogether unworthy . . . I am maggot juice, I am snail's breath.*"[9] Greg is jesting here, but he's hardly exaggerating. Consider Ignatius of Loyola's confession about himself as "a wound and ulcer," which only produces "so many sins . . . so many iniquities, and poison so utterly foul."[10]

Ugh!

## JESUS POINTS TO THE ROAD

Thoroughly unimpressed with how scholars understood humility, I turned to see how Jesus taught it. When I did, I came upon Matthew 23, and my heart roared. In one sweeping passage, Jesus waves off the humilitants, overthrows both ditches, and reveals a better framework for understanding ourselves—one that leads to security, empowerment, and confidence.

In Matthew 23, Jesus unleashes his most aggressive critique of the Pharisees. Most translations title his attack "The Seven Woes." Before his attack (Matthew 23:1–12), Jesus highlights the foundation of the Pharisees' problem: they lacked humility. Here, Jesus offers his most comprehensive and salient vision of humility, while also exposing layers of falsehood that keep us from it. He shows us the truth of what humility is, then he exposes the lies that thwart it. Realizing this humility for ourselves will therefore require both shaping ourselves around new truths and deconstructing old falsehoods.

Matthew 23:1–12

> Then Jesus said to the crowds and to his disciples: "The teachers of the law and the Pharisees sit in Moses' seat. So you must be careful to do everything they tell you. But do not do what they do, for they do not practice what they preach. They tie up heavy, cumbersome loads and put them on other people's shoulders, but they themselves are not willing to lift a finger to move them. Everything they do is done for people to see: They make their phylacteries wide and the tassels on their garments long; they love the place of honor at banquets and the most important seats in the synagogues; they love to be greeted with respect in the marketplaces and to be called 'Rabbi' by others. But you are not to be called 'Rabbi,' for you have one Teacher, and you are all brothers and sisters. And do not call anyone on earth 'father,' for you have one Father, and he is in heaven. Nor are you to be called instructors, for you have one Instructor, the Messiah. The greatest among you will be your servant. For those who exalt themselves will be humbled, and those who humble themselves will be exalted."[11]

## HUMILITY CANNOT BE THE OPPOSITE OF

## PRIDE

The first thing we learn from Jesus in Matthew 23 is that humility cannot be the opposite of pride. The humilitants are wrong. Yes, pride is bad, and Jesus exposes the pride of the Pharisees: They wanted the important seats at the synagogues and to be addressed by important titles (Matthew 23:6–7). It doesn't take a genius to understand that being given these supposedly important things might compel a person to believe they, themselves, are somehow more important, more valuable, or better than others. And this, Jesus teaches, is the gist of what pride is: to view yourself as better than others.

But then Jesus blows everything up. He adds a profound twist. It's also destructive to consider yourself *below* others. Jesus says both stop putting yourself above others by *receiving* pride-inducing titles ("you are not to be called 'Rabbi'") and stop putting yourself beneath others by *giving* pride-inducing titles ("do not call anyone on earth father" or teacher, rabbi, coach, pastor, CEO). We know the titles themselves don't concern Jesus since Jesus uses them elsewhere. In fact, even right here in this passage he refers to the Pharisees as teachers. So, the titles aren't the real issue. Jesus is diagnosing a deeper sickness. Namely, the sickness of believing yourself to be more-than or less-than others, and titles, seats in synagogues, special uniforms, and private parking spots are the artifacts of life this sickness feeds on.

Jesus agrees with the humilitants that pride is unholy. But then he challenges them: the opposite of pride is also unholy. And if the opposite of pride is unholy, then it should go without saying that the opposite of pride cannot be humility. So, the first thing Jesus does is unhinge humility from the bottom of pride.

**Pride**

**? ? ?**

Everyone agrees that pride is bad, but so is pride's opposite. This makes sense. As any psychologist will tell you, the opposite of pride is not humility, it's shame.[12] Can humility be synonymous with shame? I'd argue at the top of my lungs: NO! Biblical humility is not "self-accusation, self-disparagement, or wallowing in cringing feelings of inferiority."[13] If that was what Jesus was selling, no way would he have drawn the crowds he drew, no way would his teachings have liberated people the way they did, and no way would his revelations be celebrated as good news.

**Pride**

**Shame**

Jesus shows us that both shame and pride are assessment errors. When you're puffed up in pride and consider yourself better than others, you inaccurately depreciate the value of others while unjustifiably inflating your own value. It's an erroneous appraisal and a distortion of reality. But when you're buried in shame and view others as better than you, you are being equally erroneous. Seeing yourself as despicable is not humility. Wallowing in your inability is not humility. Self-deprecation is not humility. Humility has to be something else—and something more.

## HUMILITY OPPOSES BOTH SHAME AND PRIDE

The heart of Jesus's teaching on humility is that humility stands against the core force that produces *both* shame and pride!

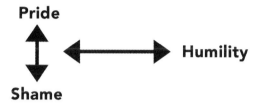

This way of looking at humility may seem confusing at first. We're not accustomed to thinking of humility contrary to both shame and pride. But it makes sense. Philosopher James Kellenberger's war analogy is illuminating. Winning a war is the opposite of losing a war. But pacifism is the opposite of both.[14] It would be silly to think of pacifism as a balance between winning a war and losing a war. Pacifism opposes war itself—it's something different altogether. Likewise, humility is not a balance between shame and pride, but something altogether different from whatever begets both.

Thinking of humility in this way revolutionizes how we look at ourselves and each other. Among other things, humility does not necessarily mean thinking less of yourself. In fact, as followers of Jesus, there must be a floor to how low we can view ourselves.

## HOW LOW CAN WE GO?

Some people—we've all met them—have grandiose opinions of themselves and seriously need to come down a notch or two. And if they were to come down a notch or two, we'd say they humbled themselves. Still other people—we've all met them, too—have such a low and despicable view of themselves that anyone can see they are acting far more pathological than holy. For them, humbling themselves might mean thinking *more* of themselves. We don't often think of humbling ourselves in this way, but for some people that's exactly what Jesus's teaching implies.

Jesus does not allow us to appraise ourselves below a certain point. Two fundamental Christian beliefs blatantly imply this basic and essential human value.

## HUMANS ARE LOVED BY GOD

In their great effort to minimize the self, humilitants come into conflict with a central teaching of Scripture. God loves us and wants to spend eternity with us. Humilitants must endorse two seemingly incompatible claims:

| | | |
|---|---|---|
| God loves me very much and wants to spend eternity with me. | —AND— | I am a worthless, insignificant zero, too small to matter, a wretched stain on the face of creation, an ulcer, a wound. |

Would God really want to spend eternity with the unlovable person described above? I'm not buying it. If God loves us and wants to spend eternity with us, there must be something lovable about us.

Humilitants will respond, *God loves us because of who God is, not because of anything about us.* This clever retort sounds highly complimentary of God, but it doesn't really work. If God's love is only about who God is, having nothing to do with us, then it's not *us* God loves. Rather, God is merely loving himself through us.

But perhaps humans shouldn't be loved in the first place. Maybe thinking highly of ourselves somehow competes with God. John Calvin seems to endorse this when he says, "God cannot bear with seeing his glory appropriated by the creature in even the smallest degree, so intolerable to him is the sacrilegious arrogance of those who by praising themselves, obscure his glory as far as they can."[15]

As religious as this line of thinking might seem, it conflicts with too much Scripture to be taken seriously. The whole reason Jesus came was because God loves *us* (Romans 5:8). Furthermore, Jesus seems to have no problem praising others. Consider the Canaanite woman (Matthew 15:28), the centurion (Matthew 8:10), and the woman with the two coins (Mark 12:43–44). Or consider the woman at the home of Simon the Leper. She commits the controversial act of anointing Jesus's feet with expensive oils. Amidst a chorus of guffaws and disapproval from the disciples, Jesus defends her, saying her act is so worthwhile that it will be told in the gospel "in memory of her" (Mark 14:3–9). Her story is to be told not in memory of Jesus or in praise of God but in memory *of this particular woman.*

God has no problem with his beloved people receiving praise. His glory is secure.

In fact, we are instructed to "build each other up" (1 Thessalonians 5:11) and to love our neighbors (Mark 12:31). Those others, including those neighbors, are people, too. If we really view them as loathsome, can we love them in any authentic way? No. Can we really build them up? Of course not. When we view ourselves too low, biblical teachings often become screwy and incoherent like this.

Many Christians come to the Ditch of Smallness, and therefore the humilitant view of humility, because of their view of sin. Since sin is detestable, and since we're all sinners, it seems perfectly logical that we are also detestable. Yet the Bible makes it clear that our sin condition, though it affects our standing with God, does not affect our worth.[16] God loved us "while we were still sinners" (Romans 5:8). Sin may be wholly detestable, but we are not.

## JESUS WAS FULLY HUMAN

The Bible tells us that Jesus was made "fully human in every way" (Hebrews 2:17). In fact, he had to be human "in every way" in order to represent us in covenant with God. If he was not fully one of us, then God wouldn't be covenanting with us, he'd merely be covenanting with himself. This explains why the Christian tradition has always defended the full humanity of Jesus with such great passion. Sure, Jesus remained God in his identity, but he "empties himself" of all divine advantage in order to live among us, as one of us (Philippians 2:7).[17]

This full humanity means that whatever we say about humans we also say about Jesus. Should we really call Jesus "a wretch, filth, far worse than nothing"? Or, "incapable of anything worthwhile in God's sight"? Of course not. We can hardly even think it. And since he was fully human, then we humans shouldn't think such things about ourselves, either. Team Smallness proclaims that being human inevitably means being loathsome. But the incarnation—God becoming fully one of us—shows us this cannot be so.

The only way to really believe that God loves us, and that he doesn't merely love himself through us, is to accept that we are lovable. The only way to believe a perfectly holy God became human is to believe that humans are not inherently unholy. Ultimately, for the good news to be true (and good), *we* can't be all that bad.

Shame and pride are dysfunction steroids. They amplify the symptoms of our most troublesome pathologies. They make our depression darker, our anxiety tighter, our addictions stickier, and so forth. So it makes sense that God would call us to humility, which, when fully realized, eliminates both shame and pride. Of course, inversely, fostering either shame or pride depletes humility. What's so troubling about the ditches is that they inevitably lead to both. The Ditch of Smallness leads to shame, the Ditch of Bigness to arrogance.

## TEAM SMALLNESS KILLS HUMILITY WITH SHAME

"I've got this knot in my shoelace," I told Mike. "Go ahead without me."

It was late summer, just before entering seventh grade, and we were all required to get physical examinations before we could play sports. The city offered these physicals to everyone on a Saturday in the high-school locker room. The seventh-graders got their examinations at 10:00 a.m., the eighth-graders at 11:00 a.m., and so on. Mom brought me to the school and waited for me outside the locker room. I was excited because many of my friends, whom I hadn't seen all summer, were there for their physicals as well.

It worked like this: Boys would strip naked and stand in a line. At the front of this line sat a doctor with a rubber glove grabbing testicles and saying, "Turn your head and cough." The line of naked boys was growing fast, so there was pressure to undress quick. Mike was clever. He wore sweat pants and sandals and yanked them off before I could even sit down.

As I was sitting, I happened to notice some of my peers had body hair! Mike had hair on his chest and above his penis—all my friends did! A dreadful revelation rose up from some cold dark place to confront me. My friends were men and I was not. I had no hair here or there and at that moment I wondered if I ever would. Something was clearly wrong with me.

I sat heavy on the bench. Mike looked down at me. "Are you coming?"

"Yeah," I said, but I had no desire to take off my clothes to reveal my childish baldness, so I scrambled to think up an excuse to buy some time. "Oh, dang it," I said, fumbling with my shoelaces. "I've got this knot in my shoelace. Go ahead without me."

Thankfully, he did, and I exhaled in relief. My next plan was to wait around for the eighth-graders. It didn't matter if they saw my hairless body. I didn't know them, and they were far older. Except I did happen to know several of them, and a ninth-grader. It wasn't until the tenth-graders arrived that I felt I could undress.

These tenth-grade guys were beasts, twice my height, and some of them had beards! But I undressed, finally, and joined the line, standing there in my smooth nudity, right between two naked men—a hairy butt at my face and a hairy crotch behind me—pondering my inadequacy. The only tree in the forest without any bark.

What was this debilitating power that pushed me around at gunpoint and compelled me to lie to my friend and wait around a locker room for several hours, while Mom waited in the hall? What was this heavy, sick feeling?

Shame.

The dread that I might be abnormal, deformed, or not as good as everyone else overtook me. Dallas Willard captures the gravity of shame well when he says, "Shame . . . is a dimension of condemnation that reaches into the deepest levels of our souls. . . . [W]e are *self*-condemned for being the person we are. It touches our identity and causes self-rejection. . . . [W]e wish to be someone else. But of course we cannot. We are trapped."[18] Yep. That's what I felt.

Luckily, my little shame experience was short-lived. But, over the years, I've worked with hundreds of people whose whole lives are marked with a tenacious proclivity for these terrible feelings. Several symptoms stand out. The first is an overwhelming self-focus. Shame rings deep, pulling our attention inward into a vacuum of acute self-awareness.[19] Everything we do takes on heavy meaning. One potential crisis after another flashes on our internal monitors. Did I say something dumb? Am I overdressed? Am I being a good-enough listener? We experience every flaw, every foible, "out of proportion with the actual severity of the event."[20] Imagine spilling your dad's beer. Okay, now imagine spilling your dad's beer when he was already very angry at you for something else.[21] Dad's preexisting anger is what living with a propensity for shame is like. It's flammable gas hovering perpetually inside us, waiting for any small failure to ignite it—magnifying every little mistake and any minor negative outcome. It's hard for the shame-prone to look away, relax, or be at peace.

This pernicious self-focus leads to a second common shame symptom: heightened social frustration. In the locker room, I didn't feel shame until I saw my friends. Heck, I could've gone right along whistling a happy tune in my delayed puberty without even giving it a second thought had I not noticed Mike and all my hairy pals. It was when I saw them that I felt I was in danger. We experience shame in relation to others, so it thrives under the threat of being discovered. In this way, shame converts others into adversaries.

The shame-prone end up in a sad trap. On one hand, they hunger for social approval—and because of their anxiety about themselves they might even hunger for it more than normal. On the other hand, this heightened desire to be liked, and the anxiety that comes with that desire, turns people off, thereby sabotaging their efforts to actually connect with others. These self-condemned souls worry excessively about being good enough for relationship, yet it's often this excessive worry that makes relationship so troublesome.

To be clear, shame is not merely guilt. Guilt is about an action; shame is about the self. Guilt is about some external and inessential thing; shame is about who I essentially am at my core. Guilt is experienced as "I *did* a horrible thing," while shame is experienced as "I *am* a horrible thing." For this reason, shame often breeds self-centeredness—because it is all about the "I" who did the thing instead of the thing done. It's also why guilt tends to be more other-oriented. Guilt often motivates repentance, reconciliation, and empathy. Shame, on the other hand, often leaves us unreconciled and has been shown to deteriorate relationships.[22]

You've probably experienced the ineffectiveness of shame for yourself. Have you ever confronted someone for some dumb little thing and ended up triggering an emotional tsunami? Like maybe you say to your friend, "Hey Margo, next time you come over to visit, please don't park on the lawn." Then, to your surprise, Margo erupts with an emotional lamentation, like, "SORRY! I'm a terrible friend, and I wish I was never born!" All you cared about was not having tire tracks in your grass, but she's gone and converted your reasonable request into this big global thing about her worth as a person. *She's* the one ruining your grass, yet *you* end up feeling guilty!

All the levers Team Smallness manipulates to combat pride are effective. I mean, it's hard to be arrogant if you've become an empty vessel and believe yourself to be a rotten worm. Unfortunately, the tactics of smallness simultaneously nurture something equally destructive: shame. In fact, when you look at the goals of Team Smallness, shame looks like the very thing they want.

But seeing our self as small does not indicate spiritual health. Rather, a small view of our self indicates a serious spiritual problem. Consider the prophet Samuel's diagnosis of Saul, who had failed to obey God over and over in his short run as the first king of Israel. "You were once small in your own eyes," Samuel told him—not as a compliment (1 Samuel 15:17). God doesn't want us to be small, he wants us to be full. In the end, Team Smallness conquers all pride, but toxic self-obsession remains—it just glows in a different way.

Given these problems with smallness, I understand the

temptation to swing in the opposite direction—as far from smallness as possible. This brings us to the Ditch of Bigness. But Team Bigness has its own dysfunction: it inevitably leads to pride (which I will often refer to as arrogance, especially as it pertains to social situations).

## TEAM BIGNESS KILLS HUMILITY WITH PRIDE

In 2006, I obtained my real-estate license. The housing market boasted jaw-dropping growth, mortgages were easy to get—if you wanted a loan all you had to do was ask nicely—and every-other person you'd meet was making fast money in the hysteria. So, with my seminary debt and a bad tie, I decided to become a real estate agent (what else could I do with a master's degree in theistic philosophy?). I studied, passed the tests, and learned the paperwork. I did some open houses and sold some homes right away. My early success was thrilling. Birds chirped, squirrels blew me kisses, and the sun bounced across the sky whistling a catchy tune.

And then the real-estate hysteria died.

At the time, it was not clear why. Banks began warning about mortgage defaults, housing prices stopped rising, and buyers became increasingly cautious. My office manager coached me to reassure my clients, "I wouldn't worry, housing prices never go down." But then they did go down. Foreclosures and abandoned homes were popping up everywhere. Entire housing developments sat vacant. Banks tightened their standards. People lost jobs, their homes, and their savings. Millions of people experienced tremendous hardship in the fallout. What happened?

It could be argued that the entire housing debacle, and

the economic collapse that came with it, was largely the result of one man: Joe Cassano.[23] When the market was good, and housing prices were growing aggressively, some investors wanted a way to make money on a possible collapse. There were no obvious ways to do this, so they created one. The scheme is complicated, and the details don't really matter for our purposes. But basically, these investors believed people would stop paying their mortgages if housing prices fell. And, if that happened, mortgage funds would fail. The investors wanted insurance contracts that would give them huge insurance payouts if a fund failed. The sinister thing was that there were ways for these investors to ensure the funds would fail (see: easy credit and no-doc loans).

The only thing these investors needed for their plan to work was a sucker willing to sell them the complicated contracts. But who? Joe Cassano at American International Group (AIG), that's who. Cassano sold contracts that said if a portion of mortgages in an insured fund failed (only 7–10 percent of them), the holder of the insurance contract would collect a huge payout. An investment of $2 million could pay out $100 million to the investor. That's a fifty-to-one return! Cassano began selling hundreds of millions of dollars' worth of these insurance contracts. Why not? He saw these insurance premiums as free money because, as the chorus went, housing prices never go down.

Not everybody in Cassano's department was so brash about these contracts. Gene Park was one noted trader who tried to show the incredible risk AIG was taking. He stood up to Cassano and tried to challenge his baseless optimism. But, as Michael Lewis reports, Cassano's division was "an absolute dictatorship," and "if you were critical of the organization, all hell would break loose."[24] Instead of taking Gene Park's concerns seriously, Cassano simply accused Park of being lazy.[25]

Cassano, his staff later reported, had a ferocious need for total control and for total obedience. He bullied and humiliated anyone he saw as defiant, and he maintained a corrosive level of fear for all who worked under him. He would stomp around the office proclaiming, "This is *my* company. You work for *my* company," and, "When you lose money, it's *my* f#@king money," and, "That's *my* bottle of water you're drinking."[26] People like Gene Park, who tried to show him how dangerous his insurance contracts were, never stood a chance.

Housing prices started going down, and the funds began failing. AIG lost billions. In fact, to avoid bankruptcy, AIG required a government bailout of about $100 billion. Why oh why didn't Cassano listen to his traders? What was it that made him so sure of himself to take such a profound risk and to ignore counsel? Arrogance.

The froth of arrogance strong-arms people into absurd conclusions about themselves, far beyond talent and abilities. The arrogant see themselves increasingly as "more perfect instances of humanity."[27] Like shame, arrogance becomes about the self as a whole. This seems to be what Cassano experienced. Cassano prioritized his own opinions and thought himself too superior to consider the advice of those around him. This is common with arrogance. It barricades the self from critical input. The more important our own opinions become to us, the less important the opinions of others become. "Treating others as if their opinions do not matter can insulate a person from others' criticisms," says philosopher Valerie Tiberius. Yet, these criticisms could be exactly what we need to be hearing.[28] When we ignore input, our hearts harden, and our exalted self becomes further and deeper entrenched in its own ineffective thoughts.

The self-esteem and positive thinking of the Ditch of Bigness effectively smites all shame, but it simultaneously kindles the flames of arrogance. This happens in a two-step process. First, self-esteem establishes the preconditions for arrogance. "You are wonderful just the way you are." Second, positive thinking shelters us from having those preconditions challenged or exposed. "Surround yourself with positive people," and "avoid negative people." Left unchallenged, we embed the idea of our own superiority, and the inferiority of others, deeper and deeper into our psyches. Then, the more we are okay with ourselves *just as we are*, the more we will locate the source of life's problems in everyone else, and the more we become, in our own psyche, better.

It sneaks up on us. The teachings of the Ditch of Bigness can sound so enlightened. As we descend deeper into it, we seem to be growing in self-realization. And maybe we are, but we are also growing in self-idolatry. We think we are strengthening our true selves—and we might be, but we are also hardening our hearts. The Ditch of Bigness inflates a hot air balloon inside that yanks every experience up through harmless satisfaction, up through competence, up through effectiveness, all the way up into toxic arrogance. And way up there lies danger, isolation, and eventual suffering.

## HUMILITY: A ROAD, BUILT ON GOD'S LOVE

To travel in either ditch is to travel in a state of insecurity that resolves itself in either shame or pride. The humility

Jesus reveals crushes this insecurity. What Jesus reveals flows from a deep and powerful reality: God loves you with maximal love. It's not possible to be loved more than how much we are loved by God. This utmost love means that we, ourselves, are lovable. And since this love for us was true while we were at our worst, and while we were against God ("while we were yet sinners," Romans 5:8), it also means that something exists within us that God loves beyond anything we do. That is, we are inherently lovable. We have inherent worth. All the woeful self-loathing a person can spew cannot alter this worth in any way.

To the apostle Paul, this love meant everything. He tells the Corinthians, "I resolved to know nothing while I was with you except Jesus Christ and him crucified" (1 Corinthians 2:2). Greg Boyd captures why Paul puts the crucifixion at the center of his understanding of everything:

> You know what something is worth to someone by what they are willing to pay for it. . . . Out of his love for us . . . God was willing to do nothing less than to go to the extremity of *becoming* our sin (2 Corinthians 5:21) and *becoming* our God-forsaken curse (Galatians 3:13). . . . God's love for us led him to the extreme of *becoming his own antithesis*. . . . God *could not have gone further* . . . that God was willing to pay the greatest price that could possibly be paid can only mean that we have the greatest possible worth to God.[29]

In the crucifixion, we find an accurate picture of God and an accurate picture of us—me and you. The crucifixion shows that you are not forgotten, God has not given up on you, God has no fear of your sin, and God does not hate you. In fact, the crucifixion reveals a God who is eager to be with you and who sacrifices everything to establish reconciliation with you. We have no choice in light of this but to reject claims like Wayne Mack's: "A truly humble person has an abiding sense of his natural insignificance."[30] To the contrary, Jesus shows us that a humble person has an abiding sense of their *unsurpassable* significance and their unsurpassable worth.

The cross leaves no room for the self-loathing of Team Smallness. A humble person embraces the worth that God has secured deep within them—a worth that does not fluctuate and does not fade. God's love establishes value that sits fixed within us just as firmly as the gravitational constant or the electron-to-mass ratio sits fixed within the universe. Whereas titles, jobs, body weight, skin color, education, and countless other shallow things differ between people, a deeper part of us does *not* differ. Call it our essence, or soul, or whatever—that pure self, inside each of us, has unsurpassable value.

This love of God, revealed in the crucifixion, cuts against the Ditch of Bigness, too. Team Bigness tries to convince each of us that we are great. Yet insecurity persists. This is because being told we are worthy is not enough for us to really experience ourselves as worthy. Even Carl Rogers emphatically believed that people need to feel inherent worth (he called it "unconditional positive regard"), but he failed to effectively demonstrate how or why we're all worthy of that. The Ditch of Bigness remains mired in an inescapable problem. As Terry Cooper put it, "We do not have the ability to grant ourselves acceptance . . . out of the depths of our own psyches."[31] We can't secure ourselves.

For at least this reason, humility requires Jesus. Without an objective referent that transcends us, like God, we have no inherent security. Without God, every morsel of security we have must be earned through our own hustle. And even then, such security remains arbitrary.

## HUMILITY: BEYOND GOODNESS AND BADNESS

Believing you are loved is not just a warm fuzzy feeling. Rather, it's a profound spiritual proclamation. Putting this love God has for us at the center of our self-assessment grounds our worth, secures our psyche, and protects us from the melancholy and the mania of the ditches—both of which put something other than God's love at the center.

Team Smallness puts sin at the center and concludes that people are fundamentally bad. But if you inflate sin and evil like this, to the point where you no longer recognize your worth or your potential for good, evil will eventually win. One large-scale example of this was the impact Calvinism had in America in the nineteenth century. This particular brand of Calvinism was a poster child for the Ditch of Smallness. "The Calvinism brought by white settlers," says Barbara Ehrenreich, "could be described as a system of socially imposed depression. Its God was . . . an all-powerful entity who 'reveals his hatred of his creatures, not his love for them.' . . . [T]he task for the living was to constantly examine 'the loathsome abominations that lie in his bosom.'"[32] These Calvinists systematized self-loathing.

The self-loathing was so intense it actually had physical consequences. Neurasthenia, as it became known, was a debilitating malaise that whittled many Americans down to morose zombies. Hordes of forlorn folks were immobilized by deep knots of anxiety, mixed with bouts of hyperanimated, ill-tempered hysteria. "Most sufferers, like [Mary Baker] Eddy, reported back problems, digestive ills, exhaustion, headaches, insomnia, and melancholy."[33] Great anxiety swept through these religious communities, bringing despair and even suicide.[34] We no longer diagnose people with neurasthenia, but many Christians in the Ditch of Smallness still exaggerate the woes of our human condition in similar ways.[35]

Team Bigness puts an ideal self at the center of self-assessment, banishing sin to the outskirts, far off their radars. Not surprisingly, they end up concluding that people are fundamentally good. But if you minimize sin and evil to the point where you no longer take corruption seriously—or our potential for wickedness—here too, evil will eventually win. One tragic example of this was Jay Austin.[36] Jay was a twenty-nine-year-old who left his office job in 2017 to travel the world on bicycle with his girlfriend, Lauren. "There's magic out there," he said, as they started their epic journey.

After months of inspiring travel and adventure, Jay wrote, "People, the narrative goes, are not to be trusted. People are bad. People are evil. . . . I don't buy it. Evil is a make-believe concept we've invented to deal with the complexities of fellow humans. . . . By and large, humans are kind. Self-interested sometimes, myopic sometimes, but kind. Generous and wonderful and kind."[37] Days later, a gang of young men in Tajikistan—wannabe terrorists—intentionally ran over Jay and Lauren and stabbed them to death.

I know how easy it is to be charmed by the many good people of the world. Take a peek at Jay's Instagram page and see how many wonderful people Jay and Lauren met along their amazing journey.[38] It's easy to get swept up in the euphoria of positivity and esteem. But evil is not make-believe. It is real.

Good and bad are simplistic categories the Bible seems to have little use for. Rather, the Bible reveals that we are loved. Not merely loved but loved by God. Humans are amateur lovers. Our inclination is to love things we consider good. So, when we hear that God loves all people, we jump to the conclusion that all people are good. But God loves both good and bad people. Look at the evaluation of the Pharisees in the Seven Woes of Matthew 23, starting on verse 13. Jesus refers to them as hypocrites, whitewashed tombs, snakes, vipers, and blind guides. They did not seem very good at all. In fact, Jesus didn't even seem to *like* them. But he did love them. God's love for us does not mean we're good or even that we will inevitably become good.

God's love blazes down from a platform of reality far higher than goodness and badness. While we are secured by the love God *gives* us, goodness and badness are potentialities placed in our laps—God *leaves* it for us. The way the Bible says it, God has *placed* before each of us "life and death, blessings and curses" (Deuteronomy 30:19). We pop into existence at the tip of a peak that descends down two opposite and extreme potential realities. We have the real capacity to become as wicked as serial killers, child abusers, terrorists, and all other such bozos. But we also have the capacity to become "good and faithful servants" (Matthew 25:23).

|  | Team Smallness | Team Bigness | Humility |
|---|---|---|---|
| You are | bad | good | loved |
| Are you trustworthy? | no | yes | unproven |
| You avoid | pride | shame | pride and shame |
| You dwell on the | negative | positive | full reality |
| Your goal for yourself is | deflation | inflation | fullness |
| This leads to | shame | pride | security |

## HUMBLING YOURSELF: CULTIVATING GRATITUDE

Humility means making God your all without making yourself nothing. It means becoming a full self without becoming full of yourself. Humility is nothing less than the calm magic of fully realizing your unsurpassable and unalterable worth. Growing in humility is growing into the reality of this worth and opening yourself up more and more to the reality of God's love for you and those around you.

To fully realize the power of this love, we must escape the Ditch of Smallness. The more self-contempt we stir up in ourselves the more we obstruct God's love for us (we can't feel both loved and unlovable at the same time), and the more we sabotage our ability to authentically love others (we won't even value our own love for others if we don't value ourselves). Concocting smallness squanders the bigness of God's love. This is why pursuing the humility Jesus teaches requires us to stop debasing ourselves. If someone compliments you for your looks, or for your talents, or for your art, or for your performance, or for whatever, you don't have to prostrate yourself in a show of lowliness. You can simply say thanks and get on with your day.

When we run from pride, we inevitably collapse into the suffocating arms of shame. "Better shame than pride," Team Smallness claims, but this is not true. Shame is not better than pride. In fact, I will argue, they are the same thing, and so they are equally dangerous. Humbling ourselves means running toward God, not running from pride. Yes, the world is full of people who puff themselves up, and plastic positivity fills our lives. But just because some people become grandiose does not mean we ought to become small and morose. The solution to obesity is not anorexia!

If you're in the Ditch of Smallness, instead of minimizing and debasing yourself, try converting every compliment you receive, and every feeling of satisfaction about yourself, into gratitude. You can be thoroughly drunk on gratitude without having a wisp of arrogance or grandiosity. In fact, the more you fill yourself with gratitude, the less you are able to puff yourself up. In that way, gratitude is a much better solution to grandiosity than self-degradation. But you have to have something to be grateful for. This means you must get good at acknowledging, and boldly embracing, everything good about yourself. You simply won't be grateful for something unless you genuinely appreciate it. Sure, you can belittle yourself to the point of tears and self-loathing, which might eradicate all pride from your life. But it will also eradicate all gratitude. You can't be grateful for something you loathe.

The invitation to run toward God also requires putting Jesus at the center of our theology. But Team Smallness often wants to put sin at the center. While every theology must account for sin, sin should not be the foundation of any Christian theology. That's where Jesus belongs. Humbling ourselves means understanding everything, including sin, through what we know about Jesus—especially Jesus on the cross. And we know that Jesus was made human "in every way" (Hebrews 2:17), and so we must admit that being human has little to do with sin. Sin misses the mark of what it means to be human and is, therefore, *in*human.

If you're tangled up in the Ditch of Bigness, you must also escape. Self-aggrandizement sabotages God's love just as self-contempt does. Like the Ditch of Smallness, cultivating gratitude is a good place to start. Gratitude has in its DNA a strong, other-oriented inertia. It pulls us outward, which counteracts the inward, self-oriented gravity of arrogance. Gratitude requires someone else. When you're grateful, your attention swells outside of yourself to the *source* of the goodness you possess. Maybe that source is God, your parents, your coach, your country, or anything else that has allowed you to be who you are and to have what you have.

Gratitude also implies interdependence. We are what we are because of someone or something else. Gratitude gets us back in touch with our actual size, our real, un-inflated self. This practice of attending to our limitations, I believe, can start to slowly work against the delusions of self-sufficiency championed in the Ditch of Bigness. And we can only learn to be okay with ourselves if we first have an accurate understanding of what we really are.

The invitation to run toward God also requires a healthy respect for the power of sin. Team Bigness often minimizes, or outright ignores, the power of sin. If we're good enough the way we are, the thinking goes, then sin must not be that big of a deal. But this is confused and dangerous. Yes, you're loved, but that doesn't mean you are good. You're loved, but you are also free. You have the real potential to become wicked and dangerous. We walk perilously close to self-destruction at all times—look at Judas, even, who walked side-by-side with history's most righteous person, yet still fell into profound transgression and moral decomposition.

## GET ON THE ROAD!

Humility stretches out before you—a road between the Ditch of Smallness and the Ditch of Bigness. It's not merely a balance between the ditches, it's a third way—it's a wholly different mode of travel. The more you learn to secure yourself by embracing the worth established by God's love, and the less you try to establish your worth from anywhere else, the more humility will flourish in your life all on its own. Securing yourself in God's love also neutralizes two of the most potent psychological toxins in life: shame and pride. Humility prompts you to fight against both shame and pride, in yourself and in others. Those drowning in self-contempt, build up. Those who are arrogant, correct. The call to humility is a call to confront both with equal passion and vigor.

Humility means putting the love of God, demonstrated on the cross, at the center of our self-assessments—at the core of our heart. With this love at the center, we are able to take sin seriously without sabotaging our self-worth or our potential for good. At the same time, we can take our self-worth seriously without being ignorant of the reality of evil or of the sad potential each of us has to become corrupt.

We hear so much about God's love, and for some people this love blows through their lives in revolutionary ways. But then, for others, God's love seems to make little difference at all. This lack of transformation has always baffled me. I mean, the profound security of unsurpassable worth, founded on God's unsurpassable love, dangles before each of us, but many do not reach out and grasp it. Why? For sure, some don't believe it, and still others might not understand it. But a bigger reason people do not experience transformation, I believe, is because they are simultaneously embracing other beliefs that compete with that love. The ditches are examples of such beliefs. Team Smallness and Team Bigness seduce us into accepting false assumptions that constrain how we view ourselves and others. And since God's love is all about us and others, these false beliefs debilitate what God's love can do.

But there's a bigger falsehood that sabotages God's love. You'll discover this false belief deep down at the root of both ditches. Team Bigness and Team Smallness both emerge from the same insidious delusion, a delusion we were all born into, and a delusion Jesus gave his life to free us from.

# CHAPTER 3.

# THE ROAD TO EQUALITY

---

But you are not to be called "Rabbi," for you have one
Teacher, and *you are all brothers [and sisters]*. And do not call
anyone on earth "father," for you have one Father, and he is
in heaven. Nor are you to be called instructors, for you have
one Instructor, the Messiah.

—Matthew 23:8–10

## RADAR ANOMALIES

Not many people can say they've saved the world from
total destruction. Lieutenant Colonel Stanislav Petrov
might be one of the few. During the height of the Cold
War, Petrov worked for the Russian military, monitoring
radar screens for early signs of American attack. Tensions
were especially high in the autumn of 1983. Russia had
just shot down a commercial airplane carrying 269 people, including 22 children and a US congressman. The
airplane had mistakenly deviated off course into Soviet
airspace. Soviet military treated the 747 as if it were a spy
plane and, when warning shots failed to deter the plane,
because they were most likely not seen, fighter pilots shot
down Korean Airlines flight 007.

Three weeks later, Russian satellites alerted Petrov of

an incoming US missile, followed immediately by four more missiles. Petrov had no time to dillydally since the US missiles would strike their Russian targets in just twenty-three minutes. Petrov was clear on what he was supposed to do. Protocol required him to immediately pick up a special phone and alert his superiors of the attack, which would then trigger an instant Russian counterattack and, most likely, global annihilation.

But Petrov disobeyed protocol, despite the radar data. Something didn't seem right to him. Maybe it was the nature of how the missiles behaved on the screen. Or maybe it was because there were so few missiles launched. Whatever it was, Petrov concluded it was a false alarm, that the data did not represent reality. He waited and, twenty-three minutes later, his judgment was proven correct. The supposed missiles turned out to be nothing more than satellite anomalies created by sunshine refracting off certain types of vaporous clouds. Crisis averted.

In Matthew 23, Jesus exposes a terrible flaw in *our* radars. We're tormented by a misguided assumption that radiates from our cores, mutates our view of ourselves and others, and causes profound spiritual and psychological disruption. Deep down, we assume that some people are better than others, and therefore some are worse.

This assumption, which most of us grow up with, happens to be foundational to both ditches. When we feel the hot loathing of shame, we feel inferior to others, and when we feel the breezy elation of arrogance, we feel superior. Thus, shame and arrogance both require a preexisting assumption that some people actually are better than others.

Jesus vanquishes this assumption when he declares,

"you are all brothers and sisters" (Matthew 23:8). We know Jesus is referring to equality here because he drops this declaration smack in the middle of his commands to not put anyone above (23:9–10) or beneath (23:8) us. To paraphrase: Don't think you're better than others, *because you are all equal*—so don't think you're worse than others, either.

Notice that Jesus does not say, "Try to imagine yourselves as equal," or, "Act as if you are equal." He asserts a fact. You *are* all brothers and sisters. You *are* all equal. Equality is reality. Which means inequality is unreality. Inequality is a sickness we must be cured of, a false hypothesis we must continually disprove both in ourselves and in the world.

Jesus tells his followers not to consider anyone above or beneath us, because it just so happens that nobody is above or beneath us. This revelation reverberates throughout the rest of the New Testament as well. Paul tells us that we shouldn't let anyone look down on us (1 Timothy 4:12), because we are not beneath anybody. Nor should we show favoritism or partiality (1 Timothy 5:21), because nobody is above us to deserve such treatment.

It may not seem like equality is real, and the data, evidence, and even our own experiences of life might lead us to think reality is anything but equal. But Jesus reveals to us that things are not what they seem. All appearances of inequality are just anomalies—sunshine bouncing off vapors, tricking our satellites.

## WHAT EQUALITY IS NOT

People can hear strange things when you say, "We are all equal." They might hear communism, hippies, socialism,

democrats, feminism, or other things Jesus was not talking about. To clear the air, when Jesus talks about our
equality, he is not talking about economics. Economic
inequality is very real, and Jesus made the poor a center-
piece of his ministry, but that is not his point here. Nor is
Jesus telling everyone at this point to sell everything they
own. Although the disciples seem to have given up everything to follow Jesus, many wealthy people Jesus met were
not asked to liquidate assets. The equality Jesus teaches
has to do with something deeper than wealth.[1]

Furthermore, equality does not necessarily mean dis-
mantling social hierarchy. Humans are inescapably hierarchical to some extent, just like most other creatures.
People with certain skills get promoted into community
roles that benefit the community as a whole. This distrib-
ution of power is natural. It should always be monitored
and those given power held accountable, but we'd be fools
to assume such hierarchies are inherently wrong. If someone has devoted themselves to understanding sewage
sanitation, let them have the power to make decisions
about what to do with our fecal waste. I don't want that
responsibility.

When declaring our equality, Jesus attacks the *exploita-
tion* of social roles for inappropriate personal gain; he
does not attack social roles per se. He assails us for puffing ourselves up because of whatever roles we have in
society. It's the siphoning of worth, the false inflation of
personal value, the erroneous inference that our social
role means something more than it does that Jesus so
ferociously attacks. So, equality doesn't mean we should
necessarily rebel against authority, or that we should necessarily resist becoming leaders. In fact, Jesus begins the
passage by defending the authority of the Pharisees,

telling his audience to listen to the Pharisees because of their position.

Also, Jesus tells us that we are all equal, not that we are all the same. We are each unique, decorated with a bounty of abilities, which are then customized in our own personal ways. The call to be equal is not a call to be like everybody else. Sure, in discipleship we should imitate others as we seek to understand and develop skills of faith. In everything else we should protect and celebrate our strange, unprecedented selves.

## UNSURPASSABLY EQUAL

Because God loves us each with an unsurpassable love, we are all equal. It's mathematical! God couldn't love any given person more than any other given person. His love for me would not be unsurpassable if he loved Gretchen more. This means we are unsurpassably equal. When God loves us with this type of love, there remains no space, no wiggle room, for us to view ourselves above or beneath anyone else God loves, which is everyone.

The apostle Paul adored this point. In fact, he even took it a step further. God's love for each of us is so great that it's not even quantifiable anymore. For instance, in 2 Corinthians 5:14, Paul proclaims, "one died for all." Jesus suffered for everyone, but this suffering was qualitative, not quantitative. He did not suffer more for you and less for me. God wasn't performing moral math—he wasn't "counting people's sins against them" (v. 19). Rather, Jesus became something different on the cross. "God made him who knew no sin to be sin . . ." (v. 21). On the cross God becomes his own antithesis.[2] And in becoming this other thing, Paul tells us, his death redeems us each equally, with equal reward ("justification and life for all," Romans 5:18), and equal standing ("the many will be made righteous," Romans 5:19). You simply cannot take Christ's atoning death on the cross seriously without also embracing the equality foundational to that atoning act.

I love how, right after Paul proclaims this justification for all, some hotshot challenges him with a purely quantitative conjecture. "Shall we go on sinning so that grace may increase?" (Romans 6:1). We're so conditioned in how we understand love and worth. We assume it must always be quantitative, that it can increase or diminish. But God's love for us, demonstrated on the cross, is qualitative. "Shall we go on sinning so that grace may increase?" Paul replies by highlighting the qualitative, binary nature of Christ's loving sacrifice on the cross. "We are those who have died to sin" (Romans 6:2). You're either dead or you're not. You can't be sorta dead or mostly dead or really super-duper dead.[3] Death is qualitative, as is God's love.

## EVEN THE DISCIPLES WERE DELUDED

The societies of the world are built around the delusion of inequality, and effectiveness here often requires us to exploit it. None of us live as if we are all equal. We each have a tenacious, deeply entrenched, preexisting spiritual condition. By the time we discover Jesus's teaching on humility—if we ever discover it through the smog of the ditches—we're already thoroughly soaked in the delusion of inequality. We've already constructed a life, a personality, and a worldview around the principles and scripts of that delusion.

Even the disciples were entangled in it. Look how preoccupied they were with knowing which of them would be considered the greatest in the kingdom. Luke records the argument occurring twice! Jesus confronts them, saying that the gentiles lord their status over others.

> But you are not to be like that. Instead, the greatest among you should be like the youngest, and the one who rules like the one who serves. For who is greater, the one who is at the table or the one who serves? Is it not the one who is at the table? But I am among you as one who serves. (Luke 22:26–27)

Jesus first calls attention to the delusion of inequality rampant in the world (gentiles lording their status over others). Given this, he asks, "Who is greater, the one who is at the table or the one who serves?" He then gives the world's commonsense answer to the question. "Is it not the one at the table?" Jesus, however, turns this perspective on its head, exposing it for the delusion that it is. "But am I not among you as one who serves?" In other words, our assumptions about who is greater are seriously flawed. If inequality were reality, then Jesus would not be "among you as one who serves." He'd be at the table—in fact, he'd be at the head of the table.

But equality *is* reality. It's just that we are far more familiar with inequality. That's what we're used to. Equality seems idealistic, and our minds become conditioned against it. We come to see equality as something that just doesn't fit here in our world but would be great somewhere like Narnia. I understand this sentiment. But I believe, even here in our inequality-bathed world, embracing the equality Jesus teaches, founded on God's love, has profound benefit. For starters, as my friend Thomas Horrocks puts it, "If we all thought this way, there would've been no slave trade, there would be no human trafficking." Thomas is right because, if the equality Jesus teaches is true, oppression is never justified.

Yet notice how each ditch fosters oppression—the Ditch of Smallness makes us vulnerable to oppression, while the Ditch of Bigness makes us oppressors.

## THE DITCH OF SMALLNESS CONDITIONS US TO BE OPPRESSED

In 1967, Martin Seligman and his colleagues made a surprising discovery. We can learn to assume we are helpless. They placed dogs in little rooms that were engineered to deliver shocks to the dogs' feet.[4] Some dogs were placed in open rooms with an easy escape, others were placed in closed rooms with no escape. When the floor was shocked, the dogs in the open room leapt out with ease. The dogs in the closed room hopped around for a while, but eventually quit trying to escape. They merely cowered and whimpered. When these cowering, whimpering dogs were later put in rooms with an easy escape, what the researchers saw surprised them. The dogs did not try to escape even though escape was easy. They had been conditioned to assume that failure was inevitable. The dogs had learned they were helpless.[5]

People aren't much different than dogs in this respect. We can also learn we are helpless and that failure is inevitable. Life can dupe us into assuming we're helpless when, in fact, we're very capable. We can be conditioned to not even try when challenges arise. Such learned helplessness is exactly where the Ditch of Smallness leads us. Believing ourselves to be thoroughly depraved and fundamentally flawed cannot lead to much else.

Imagine a young mother married to a hostile, abusive man. She toils to raise her child in the face of constant contempt from her compassionless husband. Eventually, her child sees her as her husband sees her, and treats her accordingly, disregarding her authority and challenging her at every turn. The result for the mom, of course, is horrible feelings of smallness, inadequacy, and self-hatred. She sacrifices for her child and husband, but neither nourish her in any way.

Now imagine, from this rock-bottom experience and with the last ounce of her proactivity, she seeks help. She decides to go to church, hoping, perhaps, for divine intervention, or at least divine wisdom. She finds a place in the pews and waits eagerly for the pastor to speak. The pastor clears his throat, his voice becomes animated, and he begins a passionate sermon that goes something like, "Who are we to think so highly of ourselves? Me-me-me is the song we sing. But God wants us to stop thinking about ourselves. He wants us to empty ourselves. We are to lay ourselves down as a sacrifice for others."

Our belittled, mistreated woman now feels *guilty* for even questioning the abuse she is experiencing. Not only is she to accept her smallness and humiliation, but she is to cherish it as her righteous burden. This is not a far-fetched example. Smallness theology has always been used to compel others to be subordinate, especially women.[6]

The dogs in Seligman's experiments felt helpless due to their external situation. But for those wrapped up in the Ditch of Smallness, the helplessness is internal. The futility lies within. Jürgen Moltmann sees the sickness of smallness clearly. "A human life that is denied, rejected, and despised atrophies, becomes sick, and dies." This is why people "must be affirmed, accepted, and loved."[7] Abuse and belittlement are never noble, righteous, or godly. They are always toxic. They are always sinful.

Humans have dignity and should resist oppression. What we think of ourselves dictates how we treat ourselves, and how we allow others to treat us. Imagine being hungry and someone offers you a savory, warm chili dog. As delicious as that would be in your moment of need, you'd probably reject the offer if you were wearing your finest suit or dress for, say, your sister's wedding. Why risk dripping chili and wrecking your outfit? But, of course, if you were wearing ratty old jeans and a sweat-stained T-shirt, you wouldn't hesitate to grasp that sloppy dog. You'd devour it without thought. We treat things differently when we don't value them.

This applies to people as well. When we view ourselves so negatively, why should we demand that others not treat us negatively? Why shouldn't we be treated like a doormat? Objectified? Oppressed? When we strive for utter smallness, these things seem like utmost success!

But we do have value, and we deserve dignity—which is why we all feel the impulse to protect it. Even humilitants are repulsed by oppression, though their view of human nature does little to challenge it.

Consider how Paul responds to mistreatment in Acts 16:36–37. Paul and Silas had been toiling in prison until an official comes to them with good news. "The magistrates have ordered that you and Silas be released. Now you can leave. Go in peace." Great news! A miracle of God! They've been released and will now run to their freedom, right?

Wrong!

Paul retorts, "Are you kidding me? They beat us publicly without a trial, even though we are Roman citizens, and they threw us into prison. And now do they want to get rid of us quietly? No! Let them come themselves and escort us out" (author's paraphrase). Paul was wronged and refuses to be treated less than he ought to be. He defends his rights. He defends his dignity—the personal escort is a way to redeem their standing in the community. And the magistrates respond by escorting Paul and Silas out of the city as Paul requests.

God's people have dignity and they defend it.

## THE DITCH OF BIGNESS CONDITIONS US TO BE OPPRESSORS

Our intentions are good. We don't necessarily want to oppress. The potential to oppress emerges gradually, under our radars, from four simple beliefs, the first two being the foundational beliefs of the Ditch of Bigness.

*You are great just the way you are.* We're told it's important to feel good about ourselves and to feel special. We hustle to convince ourselves of our own greatness, and, with a mix of entitlement and insecurity, we scramble to validate that supposed greatness. Then we add a second belief.

*Positivity is essential.* We're told that being positive is necessary for living a positive life and, inversely, that negativity destroys a positive life. Notice that positivity is rarely, if ever, defined. Not explicitly, anyway. We assume what it means. In this way, the meaning becomes self-indexed and unique to everyone. What's positive for an introverted librarian might not be positive for an extroverted sales associate. This is why you'll hear Democrats and Republicans, white nationalists and black liberation advocates, and people from every other contrary ideology all proclaim the wisdom of surrounding yourself with positive people.

*Surround yourself with positive people.* We're told that surrounding ourselves with positive people not only guards us from negative people, but the positivity of others can also give a boost to our own positivity. And if the positivity of others can rub off on us, then maybe the greatness of others can rub off on us as well. Thus, we're told that surrounding ourselves with better people will somehow make us better as well. So we trip over ourselves to associate with great people, that we might find inner inflation and greatness by association. We push and shove to get close to winners and to rub up against those we deem successful. And at the very same time, we're advised to distance ourselves from the wrong ones, which leads us naturally to the next conclusion.

*Avoid negative people.* Negativity is just as relative as positivity. I decide what's negative for me, and you decide what's negative for you. The joke's on us, though. Since there's no objective standard, avoiding negative people ends up being tantamount to ostracizing whoever we happen to dislike. This can be anyone who merely disagrees with us or challenges us on the simplest things. We segregate ourselves from these supposedly toxic negatives, and within the fog of our esteem and positivity, we feel wise and righteous doing so.

Listen to the supposed wisdom of our society. We denigrate others, then separate from them, all while exalting ourselves in the process. One aphorism, for instance, says, "You will be too much for some people. Those are not your people."[8] Notice how "too much" is so perfectly ambiguous and self-aggrandizing. I mean, what's more self-glorifying than convincing yourself that people who disagree with you, who don't like you, or who challenge you do so only because you are so great and are simply too much for them? Then, notice how these same people are also viewed as *other* ("not your people"), and since you are too much for them, they must be too little to matter.

A prominent English media celebrity with almost a million followers on Twitter, had as her Twitter bio, "If your friends don't like it when you have a different opinion, don't change what you think, change your friends." Obviously, this is a false dichotomy. But look at how self-esteem and positivity sabotage authentic relationship and compel us to prioritize our dumb principles over real people. "Don't change what you think," she says. Why not? Doesn't *all* growth involve a change in how one thinks? "Change your friends," she says. Why? Must we only have friends who agree with us? Must we force (oppress) them to think like we think, or else? Whenever I prioritize other people's positivity toward me and their conformity to my beliefs, relationship vanishes. Whoever tolerates such nonsense expectations is not my relationship partner; they're simply an extension of me.

It's especially difficult to escape these beliefs when we have systematically eliminated anyone who might challenge them. "Avoid negative people" we say, where *negative people* just so happen to be those individuals with the temerity to challenge our ridiculous worldview. Instead of listening to them, we convince ourselves that *they* are the problem. "They're just haters," we say. Or, as Bill Maher diagnoses it, "The most important thing is 'just you doing you'—but what if the 'you' is just a big a—hole?"[9] The unstated answer should be obvious. You continue being an a—hole.

The famous architect Frank Lloyd Wright abandoned his family and took up with a mistress. His opinion of himself, and others, made his conduct perfectly acceptable to his own mind and heart.

> I want to say this: laws and rules are made for the average. The ordinary man cannot live without rules to guide his conduct. It is infinitely more difficult to live without rules, but that is what the really honest, sincere, thinking man is compelled to do. And I think when a man has displayed some spiritual power, has given concrete evidence of his ability to see and to feel the higher and better things of life, we ought to go slow in deciding he has acted badly.[10]

Arrogance is a mindset that makes others insignificant and, therefore, expendable. It's a distortion of reality that smothers any objections we might have about exploiting others. We will treat people how we value them. Or, as Samuel Johnson succinctly warns us, "he that overvalues himself will undervalue others, and he that undervalues others will oppress them."[11] Self-exaltation inevitably cultivates oppression.

## HUMILITY IS THE ROAD

The ditches pull us up and down on terrible waves.
You are wretched and loathsome!
You are glorious and wonderful!
You're the worst!
You're the best!
"You are all brothers and sisters," Jesus proclaims, and calms the storm. Whereas the ditches each affirm hierarchy, thereby reinforcing inequality—and eventually reinforcing oppression—Jesus's proclamation of equality is a battle cry against all hierarchy and oppression.

Jesus is telling us that things are not what they seem. Someday the facade will fall, and we will all see how ridiculous the bigshots are and how perfectly adequate the outcasts have always been. We'll see that nobody deserves to be oppressed, and nobody is entitled to oppress. We'll see that oppression is a symptom of a world still desperately trapped in the delusion of inequality. We'll see that oppression and inequality are merely the anxious tantrums of a people still trying to secure themselves with a thousand strange things other than God's love for them.

In this way, humility is a campaign against the delusion of inequality. It's lifestyle warfare against the principalities and powers that exalt some and denigrate others. It's a ministry of actively redeeming the oppressed and disempowering oppressors. It's an expedition in learning how the love of God secures us to boldly engage an insecure world.

## PUTTING JUSTICE IN ITS PLACE

The equality Jesus calls us to can seem strange to us. Equality is "not sensible," laments Bruxy Cavey.[12] Yet, Jesus does not waver from his bold endorsement of it. Consider the parable of laborers in the vineyard (Matthew 20:1–16). Some of those laborers were hired early in the morning, some were hired at the end of the day—right at the point when the work was almost done! And when those who came late were paid the same amount as those who had toiled since early morning, great controversy erupts. Those who'd been there since morning were furious. "These workers only worked an hour, but we have been toiling in the heat all day, yet you have made them equal to us" (Matthew 20:9, author's paraphrase). So unfair! So unjust!

Yet we know God is fair and just. So how do we explain this?

The answer: Jesus is calling us to something more fundamental than justice. "Justice is aiming way too low," says Cavey. "Jesus wants you to go beyond justice . . . to go beyond what's fair."[13] The real sickness is inequality, not injustice. Injustice is simply one way inequality expresses itself.

Okay, yes, we need to fight injustice, too. Injustice is very real and involves a real loss. The ache of what's lost, the sharp emptiness of whatever was taken from us and is now owed to us, compels our desire for justice. We want what's lost replaced. We want what's taken returned.

Sometimes this desire can be satisfied. A coworker can replace the birthday cake he prematurely cut a slice of. That's fair and simple. Retributive justice is a philosophy that emerges from our desire for fairness like this. It seeks proportional punishment for wrongs committed.

But many of the violations we endure are permanent and unfixable, they can never be satisfied. The soldier who loses an arm in battle won't get it back. The husband who lost a spouse to a drunk driver won't get his wife back, no matter how many years the drunk serves in prison. The choir boy molested and abused by his priest will not get his normalcy or innocence back, no matter how much money the church is required to pay.[14] Retributive justice, to be frank, is an illusion in this world.

Jesus recognizes this futility. With a wave of his hand he vetoes the Old Testament's attempt at a perfectly balanced retributive justice system—called the *lex talionis*. He then replaces it with a seemingly absurd alternative, one that mocks all sense of such justice: "You have heard it was said, 'Eye for eye, tooth for tooth.' But I tell you, do not resist an evil person. If anyone slaps you on the right cheek, turn to them the other cheek also" (Matthew 5:38–39).

Jesus offers this seemingly ridiculous and foolhardy teaching as both a rejection of our futile efforts at retributive justice and as a proclamation that reality is not what it seems. In a world where inequality is reality and death is the end of our story, retributive justice—in all of its sad futility—would be the best we could hope for. But Jesus reveals that reality is not what it seems. Whenever we get hurt, exploited, neglected, abused, duped, whatever, we feel diminished. We take it personally. We feel small. But all such feelings are founded upon a lie.

"You are all brothers and sisters." The only thing you should take personally is that God died for you and longs to be with you. You are ultimately impervious to all other wrongs—as much as they genuinely hurt. So, Jesus doesn't tell us to say, "Demand repayment for our debts as we have demanded repayment from our debtors." Rather, he tells us to forgive. Let it go.

The spiritual secret behind all of this is that, no matter how perfect the justice and no matter how much recompense, a dysfunctional person will remain dysfunctional. But at the same time, a secure person, secured in God's love, will remain secure whether they ever see justice or not. Thus, Jesus, in the here-and-now, emphasizes equality.

Really, almost every injustice is a form of oppression. By telling us that we are all "brothers and sisters," Jesus shatters the foundational belief of all oppressors: some people are better than others. And when he destroys this belief, he simultaneously overthrows the ditches, each of which nurtures oppression in its own way. Therefore, humbling ourselves really is the most powerful antidote to injustice. Humility is injustice kryptonite, it's oppression poison, it's a lifestyle that fosters meaningful justice from the roots up and from the heart out.

| | Team Smallness | Team Bigness | Humility |
|---|---|---|---|
| You are | bad | good | loved |
| Are you trustworthy? | no | yes | unproven |
| You avoid | pride | shame | pride and shame |
| You dwell on the | negative | positive | full reality |
| Your goal for yourself is | deflation | inflation | fullness |
| This leads to | shame and conditions the oppressed | pride and conditions the oppressor | security and liberates both the oppressed and oppressor |

## HUMBLING YOURSELF: PURSUE EQUALITY

Humility is not just some precious aphorism to paste on our Bible covers to impress our grandmothers. "You are all brothers and sisters," Jesus says, exposing the wicked and unforgiving delusion of inequality to the light. In one short passage, Jesus shows us where we need to be and exposes what has kept us from getting there. We can now move forward, invulnerable to the wicked economy of inequality, no longer harassed by the tyrannical priorities and unnecessary anxieties of a fluctuating ego.

But we'll never truly step into this stability as long as we continue to reinforce hierarchy. For the Ditch of Smallness, this means we must change how we talk about people. We must stop talking small about them. We don't need to. Being human is awesome—God even tried it himself for as long as the world would allow it. God truly loves people, and, in fact, he still longs to "dwell among them" (Exodus 29:46). We must now stop denigrating that which God cherishes.

Some people, I think, talk small about people as a backward way of complimenting God. "God, you are so big, and I am so very, very, very small," they say, as if God were somehow bigger if people were smaller. But this is a gimmick. Making people smaller does not make God bigger. Nor does our greatness threaten God. God is secure. He doesn't need our backward compliments.

Yes, arrogant people exist, and they often carry out great oppression. But belittling people to keep them from becoming proud fails to prevent oppression. In fact, belittling people simply leaves them far more vulnerable to the very oppression we long to overthrow. If you really want to constrain the power of the arrogant, build people up! Instead of hunting for things to denigrate in people, learn to find people's strengths. Instead of lamenting people's sins, celebrate their goodness. Instead of asking things like "what do they deserve," ask, "how can I help them?"

For the Ditch of Bigness, pursuing equality means we must change how we view relationships. We must stop overengineering our connections and encounters for personal benefit. For instance, if we keep hustling to surround ourselves with positive people, we'll simply amplify the power of hierarchy in our minds.

Yes, if you want to learn a new skill, or get better at some thing, it helps to find someone who excels at that. Be selective. We also ought to be selective about who we develop close bonds with, just like Jesus did when he selected his disciples. I'm all for having good boundaries. Furthermore, I fully accept mimetic theory—the idea that we each inevitably tend to imitate those around us. Mimetic theory is our default behavioral tendency. I think this is what Solomon was getting at when he said, "He who walks with wise men will be wise, but the companion of fools will suffer harm" (Proverbs 13:20). If this was all we had to go on, the effort to surround ourselves with positive people and to associate with effective and successful folks would be wise.

Here's my problem, though. I have to balance all of that while Jesus tells me to live boldly against my culture. Jesus calls me to dwell with the ineffective (the meek), the morally compromising (the prostitutes), the greedy (tax collectors), and so forth. So, yes, mimetic theory is true, as a default. Unless given good reason to challenge the beliefs, habits, customs, and values of our communities, of course we will adopt them. But the point I'm making is that Jesus *has* given us good reason to challenge them—in particular, the delusion of inequality and the dysfunctional views of human nature we find in each ditch.

So, instead of surrounding yourself with positive people, and like-minded people, try building relationships with a diverse group of people—as diverse as you can handle. Push yourself! The more ineffective they are, and the less they benefit you personally, the better. Develop an appetite for people who challenge you. Iron sharpens iron, the proverb goes. It's the tension and friction of difference that strengthens and sharpens us, not the soft pudding of similarity. And don't get to know them just so you can change them. Sure, if you can help them out, great. But the desire to help, to be a messiah, can easily get in the way of developing skill at loving people *as they currently are.*

For sure, if you surround yourself with people just like you, life will be easier. You won't have to accommodate anyone else or make personal changes. But don't expect to be challenged or to grow as a person. Those in the Ditch of Bigness surround themselves with like-minded people because it protects their grandiose delusion about themselves. Like-minded people won't challenge the ridiculousness of each other's thinking.

To really grow, in humility and as a person, you need to be around people who challenge you, which often seems negative at first. By challenge, I don't mean someone who helps you meet your fitness goals or anything mundane like that. What I mean by challenge is to challenge things like our ability to love. Surrounding ourselves with positive, like-minded people doesn't challenge our ability to love at all. But developing relationships with people who, say, take more than they give, or people who hold opposite political views, or hostile people who smell of alcohol and don't shower regularly, *now* you'll find yourself challenged!

# CHAPTER 4.

## TRAVELING ON A DANGEROUS ROAD: ESTEEMATING

---

You may have heard the phrase, "Pride is the root of all sin." But I'd bet that you've never heard the phrase, "Shame is the root of all sin."[1] Well I'm here to tell you that both phrases are saying the same thing. I know, they seem like opposites, but in the most crucial sense, they are identical. To see this, let me tell you about Ernst and Freemont:

My friend Ernst:

> Ernst tries hard to be liked, but it's hard for him. He is short. He overeats when he's stressed—and he's always stressed, so he's a tad portly. His upper gums are too large, which makes his upper teeth look strangely small, so he avoids smiling in public. Ernst has a low bowling average and an obnoxious laugh that sounds shrill and artificial. Overall, he understands why people don't like him. Heck, he doesn't really even like himself. Ernst feels shame.

My friend Freemont:

> Freemont fancies himself an independent thinker, always striving to enlighten those around him. He is taller than average and knows his opinion has instant sway because

of his natural good looks. It's hard for him not to smile given his perfect teeth and smooth complexion. Ladies love to hear him strum his guitar, and many of his friends are important people (just ask him and he'll name some of them for you). Overall, Freemont thinks very highly of himself and considers himself a prime specimen of what a man can be. Freemont feels pride.

Both Ernst and Freemont have come to opposite conclusions about themselves. Their assessment process can be visualized like so:

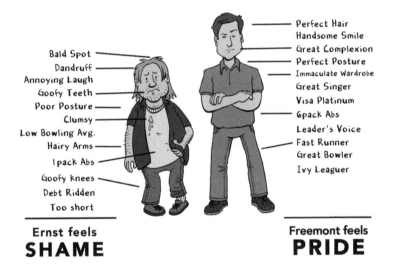

Bald Spot
Dandruff
Annoying Laugh
Goofy Teeth
Poor Posture
Clumsy
Low Bowling Avg.
Hairy Arms
1 pack Abs
Goofy knees
Debt Ridden
Too short

Perfect Hair
Handsome Smile
Great Complexion
Perfect Posture
Immaculate Wardrobe
Great Singer
Visa Platinum
6pack Abs
Leader's Voice
Fast Runner
Great Bowler
Ivy Leaguer

**Ernst feels**
# SHAME

**Freemont feels**
# PRIDE

*The math of shame and pride.*

The important thing to notice is that Ernst and Freemont are using the exact same formula. Sure, their conclusions differ, and sometimes the variables they use differ, but the math is identical. The math consists of tallying up how well they score on a range of variables. You can tally up the attributes all the way down to the conclusion. It all follows perfectly. Ernst comes to a negative conclusion and feels shame. Freemont comes to a positive conclusion and feels pride. The score of each variable adds to the previous score until they come to a total tally. They then apply that score to their self-as-a-whole. The math is sound, totally logical, yet totally opposite.

The fact they use the same formula indicates something fundamental at the core of both shame and pride. They both reside on opposite ends of the same axis. Think of the temperature axis. Hot is the opposite of cold. Yet both hot and cold are degrees of temperature. By simply adding the right kind of energy (fire), cold can morph into hot. And either one, at extremes, can be dangerous. Likewise, either shame or pride can be dangerous in the extreme. And like temperature, shame and pride can morph into one another. A shamed person can experience a change of fortune, or a proud person can have a fall from grace.

If hot and cold are on a temperature axis, what is the axis that shame and pride reside on? I like to think of it as a measuring stick we use for everything we do. Shame sits on the dreaded side of the stick, pride on the other.

Shame and pride are mathematical. Arriving at either involves a calculation, like the one Ernst and Freemont did above. I call this underlying math *esteemating*, and we all do it. Esteemating happens deep within our operating system, working under the surface, always calculating, always nudging us with results, making us cower when the results are negative, inflating us when the results are positive.

The same machine produces both shame and pride. This helps us understand why a given person can appear to have both simultaneously. "If I search around long enough," notes Terry Cooper, "I'll find insecurity beneath my grandiosity and arrogant expectations beneath my self-contempt."[2] I bet we've all seen this for ourselves. We've seen people with grandiose opinions about their own greatness simultaneously exude self-pity and even lobby others to have pity for them. We've also seen persons beaten down by their own suffocating self-contempt be bombastically judgmental of others.

Because shame and pride are the same, any given human failure can be explained by either. Consider the Old Testament story of Adam and Eve. Why did they disobey—why were they so stupid!? The humilitants blame it on pride. Adam and Eve ate the fruit because they were trying to be like God. Striving to be like God *is* pride, they say, and this pride, this urge to "exalt themselves against God," as Calvin put it, compelled them to sin.

But look how the shame narrative can explain this event just as effectively. Adam and Eve were desperate to be more like God *because they did not feel good enough about themselves the way they were.* Wanting something more and not being content with what you already have can both accurately explain an event since they are two sides of the same coin.[3]

We can now see a core reason why the struggle between Team Smallness and Team Bigness is so ridiculous. In their ancient tug-of-war, smallness advocates shout about the dangers of pride and pull us toward shame, all while bigness advocates shout about the dysfunctions of shame and pull us toward pride. One side encourages us to think of ourselves as superior ("put yourself first"), the other encourages us to think of ourselves as inferior ("put yourself last"). But "put yourself first" and "put yourself last" both assume social prioritization—inequality. In this way, both teams embrace the calculations of esteemating; they simply encourage us to bend our calculations toward one preferred outcome and away from a demonized other. Yet by demonizing either shame or pride, they reinforce the machinery that emits both. Each team, with their radically contrary ideologies, blames humanity's woes on those pulling on the other side of the rope. But the actual problem is the rope itself. And the more they pull, the more they affirm and reinforce the centrality of that rope.

The apostle Paul saw all this long ago and warned the Colossians to avoid both. "Do not let anyone mislead you, either by insisting on self-abasement [Team Smallness] or by puffing you up without cause [Team Bigness] by human ways of thinking" (2:18, author's paraphrase). Because of Jesus's teachings on humility, we now have permission, and justification, to let go of the rope. We can abandon esteemating and the psychotic game of identity calculation that goes with it.

We've already said that humility, as Jesus teaches it, opposes both shame and pride.

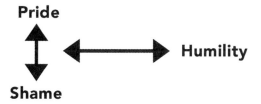

We can now restate this. Humility is the opposite of esteemating.

**Esteemating**  **Humility**

## THE DELUSION OF INEQUALITY CAUSES US TO ESTEEMATE

I've seen strange things in my twenty years of working crisis mental health. I've seen a woman with an ax who bashed in every garage door in her neighborhood, I've seen a guy who couldn't stop licking toilets, and I've even seen a man wearing an actual tinfoil hat. Behavior like this indicates a serious problem—something's not right. The person is experiencing a delusion, and they probably need help.

It's tempting to see the strange behavior of delusional people and think they are behaving irrationally. But this isn't quite true. To the contrary, delusional people are often hyperrational. Once you understand the delusional narrative, you'll find great logical coherence to the behavior. You discover that the woman with the ax really believes her children are being sexually molested in a garage somewhere. And the man with the tinfoil hat, who happens to be a brilliant graduate student, really believes the government wants to control his thoughts with radio waves from satellites, hence the tinfoil to protect himself. Delusional beliefs compel predictable, even reasonable behavior, strange as those behaviors might seem to those who don't share the delusion.

Thinking that some people are better than others, that our worth as individuals fluctuates, and that we must earn our place in this hierarchy is also a delusion—and esteemating is the tinfoil hat that betrays it. Esteemating is our frantic attempt to manage the deep insecurity radiating from this ancient false belief. When we believe that our worth fluctuates, we esteemate. How could we not? If we really believe that some people are better, and some people are worse, then we must figure out where we stand. And once we get a sense of where we stand, it's imperative to secure our standing, because it can all change for the worse. But it can get better, too, in its own pathological way. So we cogitate, perseverate, calculate, hustle to secure, then maximize ourselves.

Every person I've worked with, while they suffered under the pressures of a delusion, have been thoroughly self-focused. The delusion of inequality is no different. To whatever degree we esteemate, we become self-obsessed. "Part of what has been traditionally called 'bondage to sin,'" notes Terry Cooper, "is indeed a prison of self-preoccupation in which we are struggling to be acceptable."[1] We want to be liked, and it matters to us how others assess us. So, we downplay our troubles ("I'm fine") and exaggerate our accomplishments ("Proud Parent of a Bassoon Player"). We name-drop and strategize everything we say for a desired effect. And if the insecurity of esteemating becomes intense enough, we may even tell lies. In this way, esteemating turns everything into a crisis. There is much at stake.

But everything is also in constant flux. Which variables we calculate might change, and how we keep score is vague and inconsistent. We toil to stoke and refresh each variable, fighting against their decay (the marathon I ran last year means nothing now). Every skill must be honed and improved upon. Every positive quality must be guarded and promoted. We attend to them all and fight to secure them. We become captain of a ship with many leaks, forcing our attention to our boat instead of our journey. It's exhausting.

Everything gets consumed into the self-calculation. What does this say about me? we ask ourselves—about everything! We're all vulnerable to this, which is why advertisements are constructed the way they are. I'm just sitting here watching the baseball game when WOOSH! commercials sing and dance in my face like glowing Pavlovian bells, with each making various claims about me. The first, for beer, shows beautiful men and women who laugh and smile perpetually for no apparent reason. The next ad is for an antidepressant medication (after the beer ad, I am feeling a ring of inadequacy and melancholy). Then comes an ad offering men a pill for instantaneous erections, which I will need, apparently, if I can get my depression under control and start drinking the right beer. By the time the game comes back on, I've pondered why I don't have more friends, whether I should be happier, and whether I am sexual enough. There's nothing wrong with beer, antidepressants, or erections. The problem is our tendency to use inane metrics in our evaluations of ourselves.

Delusions make us do strange things. You see this in the Pharisees, and Jesus chides them for it: "Look at the ridiculous boxes [phylacteries] they have strapped to their faces! And look how long their silly robes are!" (Matthew 23:5, author's paraphrase). Why did these men wear such strange things? Because they presumed it verified their exalted status. The phylactery was a small wooden box worn on the forehead that held the law written on a scroll. A Pharisee wore a phylactery because it allowed them to have the law before them at all times. The length of their robes indicated the amount of education they had. The Pharisees could use these things to show everyone how much holier and how much smarter they were than everyone else. It was like saying, "Look what good boys we are! And very smart, too!" These dumb artifacts served as contrived evidence—tangible proof—of their self-inflated worth, while also reinforcing the false beliefs they so mindlessly assumed to be true.

Everything gets distorted like this in a delusion, and the delusion of inequality is no different. Certain things become way more important than they really are ("Good eye-contact is crucial to making a first impression"). Other things seem like serious threats when they really aren't (watch drivers have psychological meltdowns when some other driver cuts them off in traffic). And sometimes real danger gets shrugged off to serve the grand narrative of the delusion (watch young people trying to out-drink each other for the sad crown of Most Extreme Partier).

In the delusion of inequality, everything gets distorted, but it doesn't feel distorted. It feels normal. This is because everyone shares in the delusion. The world was already saturated in inequality long before we were born into it. By the time we first open our tiny infant eyes, the world is already horribly disfigured by inequality. From an early age, inequality is assumed in everything we learn. We pick it up from those around us. It's whispered in our ears on television and on the internet. Invisible and unvetted teachers sneak it into our system. As Camus noted, "We get in the habit of living before acquiring the habit of thinking."[5] We accept the proposition that some people are better than others long before we have the cognitive capability to criticize it. And this uncriticized narrative grows, evolves, and we don't even flinch when we hear ridiculous things, like, "You can tell he's a good man. He has a good, firm handshake." The delusion of inequality churns out preposterous principles like this, and something as inane as a handshake can devolve into a farcical inequality filter, implying some strange ladder of men, distributed up and down based on how hard their hands can squeeze. There's nothing wrong with a firm handshake, but if you're using someone's handshake to measure the quality of their character, you will end up dismissing saints and thinking highly of fools. There are, I have found, an abundance of muscular fools.

Delusions also hijack facts. Even the strangest delusions, from the ax-wielding woman to the man in the tinfoil hat, are factual to some degree. Fact: there really are people who molest children—and do so in garages, even. Fact: there really are governments trying to control the thoughts and behaviors of citizens. Likewise, the esteemating monster, and the delusion of inequality that begets him, are factual to the bone. In this land of gated communities and social-influence scores, phrases like *all the way to the top, low life, glass ceiling,* and *bottom feeder* actually mean something beyond their literal meanings.

Each and every dimension of our lives is distributed up and down on some stifling hierarchy, and each hierarchy has some bozo-in-the-know who looks down on us, through their gold-rimmed monocle, to determine our place on the strata. We have high-school diplomas, then college degrees. But that's not enough anymore because too many people have college degrees. We have master's degrees and doctorates. But now too many people have doctorates, so how are we to know who should be on top? Easy! We now have post-doctorate degrees. And the house of cards grows higher and higher.

We need the hierarchies. They serve important functions. None of them are intended to suggest a person at one level is inferior to another. They're as innocent as a handshake. But in a world so fully marinated in the delusion of inequality, things get screwy in our heads. The math gets funny. We see people differently. Not only do we value skills and assets, but we exalt the person who has them. The prettier a person is, the better they are. The more productive, the better. The funnier, the better. The smarter, the better. The wealthier, the better.

We sense there is much at stake. Michael Farr laments, "In America, being average sucks," and "average applies to most of us. But still, we fight it. We are desperate to show that we have special meaning and significance."[6] Richard Winter echoes this lament, "If you succeed, you are a hero. If you fail, you are the lowest form of life on the planet."[7] We do our best without knowing exactly what we're doing. And we're not fully sure what the objective to it all is, but we know we have to be moving up, up, up.

Inequality burbles around in our mind, messes with our thoughts, and alters our perceptions. Eventually it forces us to be sadly pragmatic. We lean toward those with more power—whether it's money-power, beauty-power, personality-power, or whatever-power, because we think they will help us somehow. Before we even realize it, we're investing more attention, more time, more energy, toward those we assume have the magic advantages. In this world, people become worth—their very lives become worth—what they can produce for us.

## HUMILITY NEUTRALIZES ESTEEMATING

Humility revolts against the world we were born into, a world where we've been raised to appraise and have lived our lives on the tottering stage of inequality. Look how backward, upside-down, and antithetical humility is to esteemating. In this life we are inherently insecure and must hustle and sweat for every morsel of fleeting security we can get. The math of esteemating operates from the outside in, pushing external scores inward. But humility starts with deep security and operates from the inside out. In a real sense, when we're humble, we have nothing to lose and nothing to gain. Humility dances under the relaxed magic of God's love, secured on the cross, and leaves us in a state of play in God's creation without the dread or deep sense of consequence so many of the world's people seem to feel.

| Esteemating | Humility |
|---|---|
| Security earned | Security given |
| Everything is considered for what it says about the *self* | Everything is considered only for the *thing* itself |
| Worth fluctuates | Worth is stable |
| There is much at stake | There is *not* much at stake |

## HUMILITY IS NOT APATHY

Since nothing affects our worth, there is a sense in which nothing matters. And since nothing matters, you might think that humility is little more than fancy apathy. While it's true that both humility and apathy cut against esteemating, humility opposes both esteemating *and* apathy. In esteemating, everything matters in a grandiose way because everything says something about who we are at our core. Apathy is the opposite of this. When we are apathetic, nothing matters in any way. But humility differs from both. Humility says that, although nothing matters to who we each are at our core, things may or may not still matter in our lives, and if they do matter, they matter only in a certain, limited way. That is, they matter only in the way they were intended to matter.

Apathy is a lazy way to soften the anxiety of esteemating. Apathy deadens all uncomfortable feelings and can anesthetize us from potential trauma (if I don't care about you, then you can't hurt me). But apathy also unplugs many of the things we need for healthy relationships. For instance, an apathetic person may very well become invulnerable, but vulnerability just so happens to be essential for trust and bonding.

As humility grows in us, as we recognize our own fullness in God's love, we become both secure *and* vulnerable. "We can be vulnerable," writes Dallas Willard, "because we are, in the end, simply invulnerable."[8] What people think, say, and do toward us can really hurt (trigger negative emotions) but cannot damage (we are still secure). Being confident in this immunity allows us to endure social hardship without choking out things like compassion, care, and love.

## HUMILITY IN THE DITCH OF BIGNESS

We've talked a great deal about humility in the Ditch of Smallness but have said nothing about humility in the Ditch of Bigness. We're now in a position to do so. Team Bigness tends to be more secular. This may be because of their repulsion to the Ditch of Smallness, which is so often religious. Whatever the reason, they seem to affirm a secular understanding of humility.

Secular researchers conceive of humility as a cluster of specific attributes. For instance, Dusya Vera and Antonio Rodriguez-Lopez suggest that if you want to be humble, you must excel at certain characteristics that make up a humble person:[9]

- be open to new paradigms
- be eager to learn from others
- acknowledge your limitations
- acknowledge your mistakes
- strive to correct yourself
- repel adulation
- avoid self-complacency
- ask for advice
- help develop others
- have a genuine desire to serve
- share in honors and recognitions
- accept success with simplicity
- be frugal

Everything on this list is glorious and should be celebrated. But it matters how we pursue these things. Secular research seems to suggest that humility results from performing well on all of these attributes. But now we are right back on the hamster wheel of esteemating. When humility is understood as an attribute, or a cluster of attributes, esteemating will intensify, and humility will become just another outside-in endeavor that we must chase—a new collection of attributes we must keep inflated.

Steve Sandage laments, "Humility is very difficult to study empirically, primarily because it is so hard to measure."[10] This fact hasn't stopped researchers from trying to measure it, though. There is even a test you can take to see how humble you are. It's called (I kid you not) "the humilimeter."[11] But the difficulty in measuring humility is not due to poor measurement tools. The difficulty is due to the flawed assumption that humility emerges from a cluster of attributes. It doesn't. Rather, as Jesus teaches, humility emerges out of an experience of wholeness, and the cluster of attributes emerges from *that*.

Humility reflects the natural thoughts and behaviors of someone who has fully embraced the reality of their profound worth in God's love. Humility is a lucidity about self and others we gain as we disentangle from the delusion of inequality. It affects many attributes and causes a certain cluster of behaviors, but it is not reducible to those attributes or behaviors. Scoring well at whatever list of attributes won't make you humble any more than surrounding yourself with laughing people will make you funny.

## THE VITALITY OF HUMILITY

In humility, we can now engage life with total freedom, without having to ask, "what does this say about me," or "what will people think?" We can be, as David Myers says, "self-forgetful" because there's no need to perpetually measure how the self is doing.[12] We can acknowledge our strengths without arrogance and face our weaknesses without shame. We can stand easy around anyone because we have a "deeper sense of self-acceptance that is not dependent on the appraisals of others."[13] That part of us that once clung to the anxious ebb and flow of inequality disengages, and we can now float over our moments with a calm immunity.

# CHAPTER 5.

# THE ROAD TO TRANSFORMATION

---

> For you have *one Teacher*, and you are all brothers [and sisters]. And do not call anyone on earth "father," for you have *one Father*, and he is in heaven. Nor are you to be called instructors, for you have *one Instructor*, the Messiah.
> —Matthew 23:8–10 (emphasis added)

In the blockbuster science-fiction movie *The Matrix*, Neo discovers his entire world, his job, his life, his history, everything, is fake. A peculiar man named Morpheus comes to him and reveals Neo's reality to be an elaborate computer simulation, then offers to help Neo escape this fake realm into the real world.

Jesus delivers a similar revelation to you and me. The world is not what it seems. There's more to reality than meets the eye. Covert forces lull us into conformity and docility through complicated lies. Like Neo, we need someone outside of the system of lies to shepherd us out. When Jesus tells his disciples, "You have one Instructor, the Messiah" (Matthew 23:10), he is establishing himself as that outside voice and declaring his unique position to help us escape. He is our Morpheus, our escape hatch out of the matrix. But we must submit to his authority and obey him.

Obey, submit, authority, conform, comply—these are modern-day cuss words! If you're like me, they make you cringe. Life is rife with hucksters, cults, and organizations that have perfected the art of persuasive brainwashing. Self-interested bozos from every direction are trying to win our obedience, compliance, and allegiance. We've seen the horrors and disastrous consequences of such obedience—we've seen the Nazi gestapo try to exterminate the Jews, we've seen Jim Jones compel his followers to drink poison, we've seen Bernie Madoff persuade smart people into giving him their life savings, we've seen the power of allegiance in horrifying groups like the Ku Klux Klan.

Everywhere we turn, persuasive personalities claim to have special knowledge or access to special truths—to get you happy, to get you rich, to get you pretty, to get you strong. Most of us have been swindled or burned. And when the hucksters are exposed, and they almost always are, the damage done is often irreversible. The time and money we invested is gone, and we're left empty-handed.

Jesus knows the world is full of hucksters, and yet he commands his disciples to teach others to "obey everything I have commanded you" (Matthew 28:20). Jesus respects our caution. He could very well be just some guy with an overabundance of charisma and public-speaking ability. For this reason, he welcomed testing and seemed eager and willing to validate his claims to every earnest seeker who approached him. Remember Thomas, unwilling to accept the preposterous claim that Jesus had come back to life unless he could feel Jesus's wounds for himself—and remember Jesus immediately holding out his punctured hands (John 20:27). Remember the early crowds, equally hesitant to accept claims of resurrection, to whom Jesus gave "many convincing proofs" (Acts 1:3)—implying the people had many perplexing doubts. Jesus expects us to trust him, and he is willing to fight for that trust.

I know, but those people were right there with Jesus. What about us?

Jesus doesn't leave us hanging. In fact, he leaves you and me the ultimate test of his teaching, and therefore of his authority. Jesus claims his teaching is so transformational that, if we follow it, we can be changed to the point that we will be able to know, from deep inside, that Jesus is not just some guy but rather a messenger from outside of the matrix. He says, "My teaching is not my own. It comes from the one who sent me. Anyone who chooses to do the will of God *will find out whether my teaching comes from God or whether I speak on own*" (John 7:16–17, emphasis added). Obedience, Jesus promises, will ignite a revolution-of-self so profound that we will see Jesus for who he really is—the embodiment of God. The proof is in the pudding, he says. Try it for yourself.

Jesus claims to be the one Teacher, and he claims that obedience will validate him (even more than intellectual knowledge will). Obedience trumps intellectual knowledge, and you find this preference stated all over Jesus's teachings—even in the verse that seems to celebrate intellectual knowledge most! "The truth will set you free" (John 8:32). This declaration comes as the second half of an if-then statement. The full statement reads, "*If* you hold to my teaching, you are really my disciples. *Then* you will know the truth, and the truth will set you free" (John 8:31–32). To hold to his teaching means to obey.

The truth that sets you free emerges from obedience, not mere knowledge. To know the truth is not merely cognitive, it's characterological.

In no way is Jesus calling us to abandon our search for truth in the world. That's what dangerous cults tell people to do. The world is full of truth, and we should seek it vigorously. Psychology, biology, physics—there's truth everywhere! Making Jesus our one Teacher is a declaration that, whatever solutions or truths the world has to offer, Jesus offers something that brings them all to completion and points them in the right direction.

It's interesting that both ditches engage Jesus in dysfunctional ways, failing to capitalize on his teachings. They each lead to different spiritual learning disorders.

## TEAM SMALLNESS HAS THE RIGHT TEACHER, BUT LEARNS THE WRONG THING

What excited me about the Bible when I first began reading it as a troubled teen was the expectations it reveals about both God and me. The Bible boldly reveals what we can expect of God, such as mercy, steadfast love, and true life. The Bible also reveals a God who has expectations of *me*. Most relevant here, God expects me to humble myself. This excited me because every expectation assumes the potential to meet it—God wouldn't genuinely expect something of me that was not possible for me to accomplish. Yet many prominent Christian leaders I encountered insisted I was incapable of meeting any such expectations. The Scriptures empowered; Christian leaders disempowered. It was disheartening.

I understand now that those leaders were trapped. When you preach "humility is the opposite of pride" and "you can't do anything good on your own," spiritual growth becomes perplexing, to say the least. The pursuit of humility becomes downright farcical. "To even ask the question 'Am I humble' is not to be so," Timothy Keller laments in his article *The Advent of Humility*.[1] Yes, even thinking about humility is prideful! How can we grow in humility if even thinking about humility jeopardizes it? According to Keller, we can't. It's not something we have any control over. And we certainly can't teach it, because "there is no way to begin telling people how to become humble without destroying what fragments of humility they may already possess."[2] Yet everyone agrees that humility is very important, so what can we do? As Keller admits, all we can do is hope that "humility just starts to grow in us."[3] Passivity is inevitable, and waiting around is the only option God leaves for us.

John Piper removes all doubt. "If humility is the product of reaching, then we will instinctively feel proud about our successful reach."[4] The implication of Piper's comments should jump off the page and poke you in the eye. God intended for us to be passive, he says, because any proactivity, or effort, on our part might lead to pride. Therefore, as a defense against all potential pride, God made all effort futile. There is no point in even trying.

Pastor Mahaney's sleep analogy exemplifies this dysfunctional view of God. Sleep is a "picture of what it's like to follow Christ" in that "no effort at supporting yourself is required," and "someone else is sustaining you."[5] In other words, let Jesus do everything.

But when Jesus doesn't do everything for us, because he never claimed he would, Christians often remain stagnant, blinking dumbly toward the sky. The church invariably gives the impression that faith must be all about heaven—some wonderful place in the future—because it obviously doesn't make much difference in this life now. This is why smallness theology so easily leads to cheap grace, and why believers who get tangled up in this ditch tend to put discipleship, and sanctification, on layaway.

Spend ten minutes in the New Testament and you'll have a hard time finding such passivity. Christians are followers of Christ, the Teacher. And although he promises eternal life (heaven), what he teaches is a dynamic revolution-of-self that starts in the here-and-now. Jesus declares: "You have one Teacher." This implies we *can* be taught, which implies we *can* learn. We don't have to let-go-let-God about everything. If Jesus identifies himself as the Teacher, then we must have the capacity built into us to discover real truths and to develop real skills.

For those of us who want to be the best servants we can be, or for those of us who are turned off by the apathy so many Christians succumb to in their smallness theology, this is great news. God made us responsible for ourselves, and like a good shepherd, he has expectations for us. Yes, our vessel is secured by God's love in all important spiritual ways, and nothing we can do can make it insecure. But we must still learn how to steer this vessel and to manage it through the waves and winds of God's dynamic creation. Humility, the proper view of self and others, is the foundation. Then, as we live this humility out, we find the way:

- to bear with each other (Colossians 3:13)
- to overcome evil with good (Romans 12:21)
- to flee evil desires (2 Timothy 2:22)
- to avoid godless chatter (2 Timothy 2:16)

- to turn away from wickedness (2 Timothy 2:19)
- to live in peace (1 Thessalonians 5:13)
- to encourage the disheartened (1 Thessalonians 5:14)
- to be patient with all (1 Thessalonians 5:14)
- to not be idle (1 Thessalonians 5:14)
- to not seek vengeance (1 Thessalonians 5:15)
- to rejoice always (1 Thessalonians 5:16)
- to respect and test prophecy (1 Thessalonians 5:20–21)
- to pray continually (1 Thessalonians 5:17)
- to hold on to what is good (1 Thessalonians 5:21)
- to reject every evil (1 Thessalonians 5:22)
- to give thanks always (1 Thessalonians 5:18)
- to lead a quiet life (1 Thessalonians 4:11)
- to control your body (1 Thessalonians 4:3)
- to forgive as the Lord forgives (Colossians 3:13)
- to love as Christ loves us (Ephesians 5:1–2)

We have much to learn and much work to do—good, fulfilling work! In their preoccupation with inability, Team Smallness conditions us to gloss over such learning opportunities. What a waste! Be skeptical of any leader who teaches that you are incapable of doing something Jesus commands you to do. When Jesus tells us to do something, he means it.

## TEAM BIGNESS CAN LEARN, BUT FOLLOWS THE WRONG GUIDE

It was in the kitchen that I realized I needed help. I was standing there staring at my foot. I had placed my foot on a square tile, being sure not to touch the seams. Then I stepped the other foot forward into an adjacent tile. Then I stepped both feet back, or over to different tiles. When I realized what I was doing, I was already twenty minutes late for work. My car keys were in my hand and my coat was zipped up, ready to go. I kept getting lost in numb trances like this. A young woman I thought would someday be my wife had dumped me. My mind would get stuck in these hypnotic loops, and I would gnaw on the same tired thoughts, all of them revolving around the same nauseating mystery of what was wrong with me, and why she didn't want me. I was a mess.

I decided to go see a counselor. I found someone offering a free thirty-minute consultation, made an appointment, then went to his office. He was this John-Denver-looking guy named Gary. His office had a couch, a swivel chair, and (I kid you not) a poster of Carl Rogers on the wall. At first, I tried telling him about being dumped, but he wanted to know about me. All I cared about was what was wrong with me and why my relationship failed, but he kept interrupting me, "Tell me about your family," and "What was your childhood like?" Though unimpressed with his customer service, I decided to humor him and tell him all about how I grew up with a young mom and about all the schools I went to and about all the places we moved to and so forth and so on. I spoke fast because I wanted to leave time to talk about my broken heart.

He said, "It sounds like you never had the chance to establish any serious roots."

The moment he said that, I felt this glacier-like thing crack inside me, and I began weeping like a toddler, blowing snotty grief-goo into tissues from the box. Five tissues, six tissues, by the seventh tissue, I started to gain composure. The crying stopped. I stood up, feeling a euphoric exhaustion, and looked down at him with puffy eyes and a relieved smile.

"Thank you so much," I said, as I stepped toward the door.

"But you still have fifteen minutes left," he said.

With a shrug, I replied, "I think that did it. I'm good." And I was good. I felt great, and I never cried about her again. Gary's insight about not having formed roots helped me make sense of many pervasive struggles in my life, including many of my nuanced anxieties, and many of my idiosyncratic self-doubts. The right insight can be powerful.

And yet, people can get lost, and stuck, in the realm of insight and never move to a stage where they change. The hunt for insight can be endless. Classical psychoanalysis was known to sometimes go on for decades, with each session being a long and tedious affair. Some of these sessions could take hours, with patients talking practically nonstop, with only occasional, carefully worded nudges from a therapist (who would take great care not to transfer any insight that came from themselves). The goal was always to have every insight emerge purely from within the patient.

When we believe every important truth lies within, our own inner life inflates in importance. The inner life becomes more alluring, captivating, even. It all contributes to a fantasy of psychological complexity—that we each have some perplexing inner labyrinth with endless fascinating passageways and fascinating artifacts constantly unfolding within. It all fosters a fascination with our own inner selves, as if we had some magic garden inside. The journey into this supposed magical self can be addicting. The payoff is when we gain a new insight—like when we learn something new about ourselves, recognize a new pattern about how we live, or discover the source of a feeling. And, to be clear, these insights can be very helpful—the one I received helped heal my broken heart. So they do have value.

But real, substantial growth comes from something greater than personal insights and from something beyond understanding ourselves. Real growth and change result from understanding *someone else*. Suppose you have financial woes, and maybe you have declared bankruptcy. Hanging around other bankrupt people might fill your heart and soul with buckets of understanding, but real growth will only come when you can learn from someone who is not bankrupt, and who is effective with their finances. To really grow, in other words, you often need to find a teacher. For this reason, the best counselors listen, offer insight, and also teach important life skills. Self-esteem, and the promotion of the self as the primary source of important truth, sidetracks us from the source of real growth.

Positive thinking can also be counter-therapeutic. Working in a mental health hospital, you find the *Stay Positive* message everywhere you turn. It's not part of the formal treatment plan, but it's uttered by nurses and orderlies and chaplains and occupational therapists. Nursing station posters praise positivity, coloring sheets flaunt it, and visitors bring T-shirts and teddy bears with positivity branding all over them.

But forced positivity can blind us to reality. It can thwart learning, especially learning from our suffering and from the consequences of our actions. When we force positivity, we force ourselves into a fake world—one that often fosters, eventually, greater suffering. I've seen it a thousand times. I've confronted people withdrawing from an alcohol or drug binge, people who've lost jobs, spouses facing divorce because of sexual affairs, criminals caught in the act, and so much more. When I ask them, "What are you doing about this?" most of the time they reply with the same sad, powerless refrain. "I'm trying to stay positive."

No! Stop trying to stay positive! Things are not okay!

We will never make radical, difficult changes if we bury the suckiness of our lives under a cloak of positivity. We'll never awaken from our intricate systems of self-denial if we stay positive. A cold splash of negativity is what we often need, especially when we're doing destructive things. We need people in our lives who are connected to reality, people with the compassion and temerity to say, "Stop that!"

Suffering sucks, but there are often valuable lessons within it. The stomachache helps motivate us to not eat too much sugar, the sleepless night warns us of our caffeine consumption, and the hangover alerts us to the not-so-fun consequences of drinking too much alcohol. The rejection of a friend might teach us not to be so mean with our teasing. The anxiety of unemployment might teach us to take our next job more seriously and not call in sick so much. Many are the lessons of suffering.

Sometimes we suffer for things done to us, for things not our fault. Even then, there are things our psyche and soul need to grieve and suffer. I've worked with many adults wrestling through the arduous suffering of being sexually abused as children. Such a traumatic violation brings many tentacles of hurt, each one requiring tremendous processing. Some feel responsible for their abuse when they shouldn't, some feel guilt and self-hatred for any pleasure experienced in the event, some wrestle with violent revenge fantasies, some wrestle with urges to violate others, and all of them must relearn about their own sexuality from a now-shattered foundation. People do heal from sexual abuse, but there are no short-cuts—including, especially, positive thinking.

As good as positivity might feel, for the most part, it is powerless. Positivity won't help you when you're unemployed, but job skills and a good work ethic might. Positivity won't help you with your marital problems, but learning to be a better communicator might. Positivity won't help you with your alcohol addiction, but treatment and healthy relationships might. Oh, and the last thing a suffering person needs is for some wide-eyed helper to tell them to turn that frown upside-down. What we most often need is not positivity, but real truth, comfort for our real pain, and real, tangible skills—things we need taught to us. We need a teacher.

We are loved, but we are not complete. God is inviting us to submit ourselves to one Teacher. Obeying the voice inside of you can't possibly lead you to growth. It can only reinforce the source of the voice: you! It can only make you more and more of what you already are! Insight and understanding are important, but the magic lies in something outside ourselves. God is calling us to become citizens of an advanced community, and we still have many things to learn—things not inside of us but out there where our Teacher is.

|  | Team Smallness | Team Bigness | Humility |
|---|---|---|---|
| **You are** | bad | good | loved |
| **Are you trustworthy?** | no | yes | unproven |
| **You avoid** | pride | shame | pride and shame |
| **You dwell on the** | negative | positive | full reality |
| **Your goal for yourself is** | deflation | inflation | fullness |
| **This leads to** | shame, powerlessness, and passivity, and it conditions the oppressed | pride, powerlessness, and passivity, and it conditions the oppressor | security, empowerment, and proactivity, and it liberates both oppressed and oppressor |

## HUMBLING YOURSELF: CULTIVATING A TEACHABLE SPIRIT

Humility involves submitting to the right authority and orienting ourselves around his teachings. If you're in the Ditch of Smallness, this means accepting your ability to learn. Team Smallness enthusiastically looks to the right authority (Jesus), but since they doubt their ability to learn, they often squander that submission. They assume they can't learn, and so they often don't. But we *are* capable of learning. If we weren't, Jesus would not have told us to submit to him as teacher.

So, in humility, we can stop dwelling on what we can't know and start exploring what we can know. We can engage our Lord not with resigned hope that he will install truth in us but with confident curiosity of what marvelous truths he has to teach us.

More than that, since Jesus gives himself the title of teacher, learning must now be considered a good thing. In humility, we celebrate questions, we pursue answers, and we encourage all desire for knowledge. This means we encourage our brothers and sisters to learn. We praise their growth and development. Sure, such praise could compel them to become arrogant, but if they do, that's no reason to fall to pieces. Challenge them. Correct them. Trust in their ability to learn. Don't *fear* arrogance, *learn* how to deal with it.

Team Bigness believes in their own ability to learn. Unfortunately, they look to the wrong authority. Instead of submitting to Jesus, they often get lost in the dull labyrinth of themselves and end up nowhere. When we consider ourselves ultimate, and believe truth lies within, our whole energy flow originates in our own ego and overflows onto everyone around us. We stoke self-esteem and positivity within, then pour all that out on whatever circumstance we find ourselves in. The call to humble ourselves is a call to change our flow, to open ourselves up to how others can shape us, especially how our one true Teacher can shape us.

We fabricate most of our self-esteem and positivity. Sure, we believe it all might eventually lead to actual esteem and positivity, but it starts out as a bold exertion of hot air, sort of a push-start on the reality we'd like to see. We want to bring about a certain reality, somehow, by pretending it's already here. Submitting to Jesus as teacher requires us to get real. In humility, we can stop borrowing future esteem by pumping ourselves, and others, up with hollow compliments. Rather, in the authenticity of humility, we now boast about actual skill development and actual learning. In humility, we praise real things.

We also don't have to pretend life is going swell when it sucks. We can dwell with people in whatever way the moment dictates. "Rejoice with those who rejoice; mourn with those who mourn," the apostle Paul says, "live in harmony with one another" (Romans 12:15–16). In humility, we can let each moment be what it is. We can stop trying to force every situation to be positive. Always being positive is inauthentic, and that phoniness will atrophy the spiritual muscles necessary to deal with the very real and dark realities of life. We don't have to hide from it under our cape of positivity. Suffering is real, but we can handle it. Not only can we handle whatever the moment brings, we will also experience an authenticity that has a joy of its own, a joy that is more invigorating than whatever positivity we might have conjured.

When we submit to Jesus as teacher, we declare that we are not already there. Sure, we are already loved, but we are not yet what God wants us to be. There is no predefined "you" deep inside trying to get out. There is only the you that you create in the furnace fires of life and relationship. Real goodness, and the guidance to get there, is found only with God, not inside ourselves.

## GET ON THE ROAD!

The shepherd has welcomed you into the flock and has brought you to his plush pasture, rich with learning opportunity. He waits nearby, watching, leaning upon his staff, eager to see what you will do with all the potential he has placed before you. Whatever you do, don't empty yourself—fill yourself! Satiate yourself in knowledge and wisdom. Seek out and take hold of the great bounty, the magnificent treasures God has left for you in the nooks and crannies of his plentiful pasture. The humble don't empty the self or inflate the self. They master the self—not because they have to but because they can, and because it pleases their teacher, who stands nearby, eager to help.

# CHAPTER 6.

# THE ROAD TO EMPOWERMENT

For those who exalt themselves will be humbled, and those who *humble themselves* will be exalted.

—Matthew 23:12 (emphasis added)

I barely graduated from high school, finishing with a D average. My problem was that I got a big thrill out of skipping classes. My final semester, senior year, was the best. My beginner's weightlifting class fell between study hall and lunch, so by skipping this one class I was able to get three hours off every day. It was a beautiful situation that I fully capitalized on.

I did go to the first day of class. I remember it because the teacher gave each student a full case of Reese's Peanut Butter Cups. He was trying to raise money so the weight room could get new mirrors. I took my box of peanut butter cups, tossed it on the passenger seat of my truck, and never went back to weightlifting class the rest of the semester.

It happened to be the heart of January, the coldest month of the year. That box of peanut butter cups froze solid within hours. Here's something you should know: There are few things in this life more delicious than frozen peanut butter cups. Over the next several weeks, I ate the whole box—50 king-sized bars, 200 cups, 17,400 calories. It cost me $100.

Graduation day arrived, and I was given my report card. There, next to beginner's weightlifting, was a thick red F. The scarlet letter floated up off the page and levitated in front of me, then began draining the vitality from my spirit. I stood there in my graduation robe like a speedbump as all the more adequate students rushed around me. I was devastated. The F meant I wouldn't graduate.

Through the crowd of black robes, I spotted my teacher chatting with someone near the flagpole. I hurried over to him and said, "You gave me an F."

"You were never there," he said.

It was a fair point, but I pleaded my case anyway. "I know I missed some classes, but I came in after school all the time to lift weights, and I'm not asking for an A, I just need a D– so I can graduate with my friends."

He adjusted his cuffs, squinted toward the sun, then looked at me with a faint smirk. "Well, I suppose you did sell more peanut butter cups than anyone else. Okay."

My abounding neglect and apathy should have thwarted my graduation, but I got lucky.

Eventually I went to college and became an A student. Much of the credit for this transformation goes to C. S. Lewis. Up until my graduation, my thinking had been becoming increasingly nihilistic. Nothing seemed to matter. It was hard for me to care about anything since we all die, and everything comes to nothing in the end.

Folks at church claimed that everything matters when we believe in God. I wanted badly to believe this, but these unanswered questions held me back. I wanted to know why we should trust the Bible or believe Jesus is God. I wanted to know how to make sense of evil, what to do about evolution, how to make sense of the Trinity, and many other basic faith questions. But my church disappointed me. They were pietists who distrusted reason. Every line of questioning eventually led to a similar, disheartening response. "You just have to have faith," or "God is beyond our understanding," or "A finite mind cannot comprehend an infinite God." In other words, there's no point in pursuing these questions. You can't know.

Then someone gave me a copy of *Mere Christianity*, by C. S. Lewis, and I felt new lobes of my brain power on. That tattered little book offered coherent answers to many of my nagging questions. I carried it with me all summer. Lewis's particular answers didn't even matter to me as much as the fact that he was taking the questions seriously. Lewis's work was a resounding affirmation of my hunger for answers, and I came to believe that God made sense and that I was capable of understanding. With that, my heart burned, my mind opened, and learning mattered in a new and exhilarating way.

Believing I was capable energized me with something like a fever. An appetite and urgency for knowledge overthrew my life. The more I learned the more I wanted to learn. I couldn't stop and decided I had to figure out how to get to college. With my high-school grades, this was tricky. Fortunately, Bethel University accepted me on what they called *academic probation*. This meant they gave me one chance to prove my academic worth. I couldn't screw up. When they let me in, I devoured everything I could, graduating three years later with almost perfect scores. It's amazing what we can do when we believe doing something matters and that what needs to be done is doable.

## HUMILITY IS CHOSEN

Jesus implores his followers to "humble yourselves," which is a blatant affirmation that humility is ours for the taking. If we so choose, we can do it.

We are not God, of course. Some things we cannot do. Salvation, for instance, is something that God does for us (Philippians 2:12). Nor can we secure our own worth out of the depths of ourselves. Fortunately, our God has established this worth for us as well, on the foundation of his great love. Many are the things God has done for us.

But humility can't be outsourced to God. "Humility is willing," says John Dickson, who has studied biblical humility more than any other scholar I know. "It is a choice. Otherwise it is humiliation."[1] I humble myself, you humiliate me. They're not the same, humility and humiliation. This is why Matthew 23:12 uses the active verb when Jesus commands us to "humble yourselves," signaling that this humility is up to us.[2] We are responsible for bringing it forth. Jesus does, however, unveil a more passive alternative—say, for those who wait around hoping humility might start to grow in them magically. "You will be humbled." Which is to say, you will be humiliated.

You might assume that Christians would celebrate such an empowering teaching. You'd be wrong. To my surprise, the thought of being proactive and capable of choosing humility is unpalatable to many Christians. A great many Christians, especially humilitants, develop a terrible spiritual habit of proclaiming, "I can't." The reason for this is that proactivity implies inner resources and abilities that we can trust. But self-trust, to these Christians, is not a good thing. In fact, self-trust is the foundation of pride! Pride, warns Jones and Michael Fontenot, almost always involves "an attitude of self-suf-ficiency and independence."[3] Therefore, since self-suffi-ciency is the foundation of pride, humility must be under-stood, to them, as the opposite, as "the place of entire dependence on God."[4]

Perhaps this mindset fuels Mark Talbot's view of his own disability. While swinging on a rope like Tarzan, Tal-bot fell and was paralyzed from the waist down. He was only seventeen. In reflecting on his horrible injury, Tal-bot claims, "My continuing disability was the chief means by which God kept blessing me." How in the world could paralysis be a blessing? Talbot explains that, through his paralysis, "God is protecting me from idolatrous self-suf-ficiency by taking various goods away from me," and, "each morning . . . my disability prompts me to trust God rather than to rely on my own strength."[5]

According to Talbot, his paralysis is a gift from God. I can't help but wonder, if paralysis is so good, then what is evil? If God paralyzes and disables us, what does Satan do? But I'm biased. I believe God grieves Talbot's injury, and that God wants Mark Talbot back on the rope, swing-ing like Tarzan again, overflowing with exhilaration and vitality.

Jesus's command to humble ourselves is an empower-ing theology-of-can that confronts the theology-of-can't nurtured in the Ditch of Smallness. Jesus gave us work that only we can do, so not all self-sufficiency can be considered unholy. At least some self-sufficiency must be good.

And it's not only Jesus. In Deuteronomy, Moses fights against these same rampant presumptions of powerlessness—you can almost hear the Israelites pestering him with meek resignations. "We are but small humans, what can we do?" and "We must wait for God to make us obey." Listen to Moses's frustrated reply.

> For this commandment I give you today is not too difficult for you or beyond your reach. It is not in heaven, that you would need to ask, "Who will ascend into heaven to get it for us and proclaim it, that we may obey it?" And it is not beyond the sea, that you would need to ask, "Who will cross the sea to get it for us and proclaim it, that we may obey it?" But the word is very near you, in your mouth and in your heart, so that you may obey it. (Deuteronomy 30:11–14)

## HOW DO WE TRUST GOD?

The core posture of the Christian is to trust God. However, when humilitants tell us to trust God, they tend to leave out a crucial piece of information.

Trust God *to do what?*

According to humilitants, we can't trust the self—not for anything. We must therefore trust God to do everything. We trust God for salvation, sure, but also to find us a job, secure us a spouse, and so forth. Taken to the extreme, we might even assume God will pay our bills, protect us from criminals, and find our lost car keys.

But "humble yourself" flies in the face of such comprehensive understandings. My own assumption is that we are to trust God *totally*, but only for those *particular* things that God wants to be trusted for. We trust, for instance, that God is who the cross reveals him to be. We trust what God says about his people: We are loved and worth the death of his Son, yet we also must repent from our sins. We trust God's promises—of our forgiveness, of our eternal life, of the renewal of the earth, and so forth. We trust God's promises of salvation and his victory over death. And, most relevant here, we trust in the resources God has given each of us to humble ourselves—and to do everything else God expects of us.[6]

God trusts people. It sounds crazy, I know. But even the Bible didn't flutter into our laps on glowing wings. Rather, God's people forged and proctored it. To say, "I trust the Bible" is tantamount to saying, "I trust the accounts of these sixty-six or so authors and the community that preserved those accounts." And when we step inside the Bible, we see God trusting his imperfect people over and over again as well, from the insecure Moses to the impatient Abraham, from the troubled Job to the fickle Peter. Each of these bumbling believers eventually came to a point where God affirmed them and declared his trust in them. If God trusts us, then it seems most sensible to presume that we might be able to trust us, also.

When Jesus tells me, "humble yourself," I realize that true trust in God must mean trusting the resources God has already equipped me with. Watch for this in Jesus's parables. Many of them follow a distinct pattern. One figure who represents God (landlord, master, father, bridegroom) is juxtaposed against others who represent us (workers, farmers, virgins). Each of these parables reveals a God who, in some sense, withdraws from his people, leaving them each to their own God-given resources. Then God returns to see what they have done with those resources.

Consider the parable of the bags of gold in Matthew 25. Here, God (the master in the story) goes on a journey (withdraws). He gives power (bags of gold) to three of his servants. He then returns to see what his servants did with the power they were given. Two servants invested their gold, the other buried his. Now, from the trust-in-God-for-everything perspective, the worker who buried the gold should be praised because, instead of relying on his own self-sufficiency, he trusted fully in God. But this is not how the story goes. God praised the two servants who took personal initiative, made personal decisions, relied on their personal capacities, and invested the gold. The servant who buried the gold was scolded! What God gives to us he expects us to use.

God calls us to be humble. He places the burden of responsibility on us. He assesses us for it. He gives wisdom (James 1:5), and he searches for humility (Isaiah 66:2).[7] Of course, God also actively humbles people, but that is humiliation and you don't want any part of that. The incredible reality is that God has really given us *us*. You are really yours, and I am really mine. God has given our self to ourselves and is waiting to see what we are going to do with what we are given. Yes, God is active in our lives. But God's hands are also withdrawn, and he watches, like a good shepherd, to see what *we* will do.

In this way, humility is empowering, proactive, and capable. As radically antithetical as the ditches are to one another, it's curious how they each end up in the same sad place: powerless, helpless, and passive.

## PASSIVITY IN THE DITCH OF SMALLNESS

The deeper you go into the Ditch of Smallness, the more passive you become. This is because the more effective you are at belittling yourself, the more helpless you will believe yourself to be. And the more helpless you believe yourself to be, the less sense it makes to even try. This is the sad song of smallness. The more you truly believe you can't, the more you don't. And the more you don't, the more you won't.

You've seen this transition from helplessness to passivity for yourself if you've ever driven your car on ice and lost control—especially if you've crashed. There is an interesting tipping point in how these events are experienced. At first, when we feel the car sliding, we try everything we can to avoid the crash. We slam the brakes. We yank the wheel. We lean strategically away from impending objects. There's a point in these events where we realize nothing we are doing is going to prevent the crash. At this distinct point, we cease all active tactics and shift to self-defense. We grab the armrest. We extend our legs. We hold our arms in front of our face. We transition instantly from an active effort-to-solve to passive self-defense. This shift to defensiveness is a clear indicator that we feel helpless. And when we feel helpless, we stop trying.

This is where humilitants get stuck. Nobody explicitly supports passivity—especially in the face of abuse or oppression. As Jones and Fontenot say, "Humility is not passiveness," and being humble "does not mean becoming a doormat."[8] But they fail to explain why a desperately wicked, less-than-zero, incapable person ought not to become passive and ought not submit to the abuses of oppressors. Do we really expect a less-than-zero to be proactive? Dynamic? If they could be, then they wouldn't be so despicable. To a person striving to be less-than-zero, passivity seems inevitable.

Jones and Fontenot deserve some credit for trying to explain it, though. They say that humble people "will

understand that on their own they cannot act wisely, but
. . . with God they can act in powerful and decisive ways."[9]
In other words, humble people must wait for God to act.

This is passivity! Make no mistake, *waiting for someone else to do it* is exactly what passivity is—even when that someone else is God.

But Jesus's words ring in our ears: "Humble yourselves." God calls nobody to sit on their hands and wait. God calls nobody to bury their gold. He prompts us to act. And the apostles echo this emphasis on proactivity. Peter, for instance, tells his readers to "clothe yourselves with humility" (1 Peter 5:5), not simply to wait around for someone else, such as God, to make us humble—or does God put your clothes on for you? The apostle Paul even had the gall to proclaim his own humility when he told the Ephesian leaders, "The whole time I was with you . . . I served the Lord with great humility" (Acts 20:18–19).

Most of us are not in some pride-induced trance, wickedly driven to glorify ourselves. Rather, most of us are simply trying to be the best we can be and to take full advantage of this incredible gift that God has given us. We desire to be effective in our walks with God. We want to grow in Christ-likeness. We want to overcome sin and failure and to become compatible with life in God's kingdom. We desire to be "good and faithful servants" (Matthew 25:23). Jesus wants us to humble ourselves, and we have the capability to do so sewn into the fibers of our bones, radiating through our flesh. He is calling us to take hold of that power and to make it real. This doesn't mean it's easy or that it's a one-time thing. Jesus doesn't say anything about how difficult it is. He simply tells us to make it happen—which implies that we can make it happen.

## HELPLESSNESS AND PASSIVITY IN THE DITCH OF BIGNESS

The rah-rah of bigness deflates our motivation, leaving no incentive, no fire, to push through the real frustration and real difficulty of real growth. The more we believe we are wonderful just the way we are, the less sense it makes to endure the struggle of growing into something more. Not only that, Team Bigness coaches us to maintain positivity no matter our circumstance. But this sabotages growth as well. The more we think our circumstance is positive, the less motivated we will be to change it. Watering the seeds of self-esteem and positivity nourishes a flower of passivity. Life goes right on evolving all around us, but we remain blissfully stagnant.

For those of us raised under the ideologies of self-esteem and positivity, we've incurred similar wounds. Informed repeatedly of our greatness and warned constantly of the evils of negativity, we've developed mastery of one cluster of irrelevant skills: liking ourselves and being positive. There's not much we can do with that, and this powerlessness hurts. But the pain is hard to articulate through our constant positivity. Some, perhaps the wiser among us, abandon self-esteem and positivity altogether and throw themselves into more productive mindsets. Others conclude what we need is *more* positivity and self-esteem.

To meet this demand, self-proclaimed gurus twist self-love and positivity into programs, courses, and informational products, which they peddle at conferences, seminars, and workshops. Many of these performers simply peddle recycled platitudes and principles extracted directly from the Ditch of Bigness. Customers are told how great they are and how much power they have inside—the teachings rarely get much deeper than that. And what can we do with all these flattering teachings? Not much, other than become gurus as well. Barbara Ehrenreich, in her book *Bright-Sided*, sees the gurus' predicament. "There's not much else for them to impart . . . they don't have anything else by way of concrete skills to offer."[10] Customers end up drinking more of the very medicine that made them sick in the first place.

Self-love and positivity can be stretched to eye-popping extremes. Dr. Sue Morter proposes that we can have "infinite power" when we attune ourselves to the rhythm of the universe. Morter's website even suggests that external reality itself is "generated" by each of us to "reveal some part of myself to me that I wasn't aware of before," and, she adds, "I assure you that's exactly what is happening."[11]

Joe Vitale claims to have coerced people into buying his products by merely "loving each name" on a mailing list. It's no surprise that Vitale was a noted contributor to *The Secret*, Rhonda Byrne's international blockbuster book, which claimed to show how the universe is subservient to the power of our thought. Health and wealth result not from skill, conduct, or providing value but from how we think about the universe. At a party bursting with people who lacked valuable skills but who felt really great about themselves, *The Secret* was like the light of God. Everything you need is already inside of you!

Not everyone in the Ditch of Bigness gets sucked into these absurdities. But the grandiose promises and candy-coated metaphysics of these gurus emerge from the conceptual foundations of the Ditch of Bigness. The ditch, which says "you are great, and you have power," is simply stretched to the ridiculous extreme: "You are really great (maybe even divine) and have amazing powers (maybe even supernatural)." The Ditch of Bigness is a rich soil that can bring forth many strange and intoxicating fruits. Yet, Jesus's words disrupt our delusions of grandeur: humble yourselves. We are not already there. We have work to do. Jesus proclaims that we *can* trust ourselves, and Team Bigness affirms this emphatically. Unfortunately, they simultaneously sabotage what we should trust ourselves to do. Jesus's teachings reveal that we can trust ourselves to become humble, Christ-like, *agape* lovers. But we are not the source of this light, we are merely carriers. This light does not ignite by simply looking inside ourselves; it ignites when we are oriented to something outside of ourselves.

| | Team Smallness | Team Bigness | Humility |
|---|---|---|---|
| **You are** | bad | good | loved |
| **Are you trustworthy?** | no | yes | unproven |
| **You avoid** | pride | shame | pride and shame |
| **You dwell on** | negative | positive | full reality |
| **Your goal for yourself is** | deflation | inflation | fullness |
| **This leads to** | shame, powerlessness, passivity, submission to authority, and feeling like you can't do anything, and it conditions the oppressed | pride, powerlessness, passivity, opposition to authority, and feeling like you don't need to do anything, and it conditions the oppressor | security, empowerment, proactivity, engagement with authority, and choosing humility, and it liberates both the oppressor and the oppressed |

## HUMBLING YOURSELF: CULTIVATING FORGIVENESS

The ditches lead us to passivity and powerlessness. But humility empowers. The ultimate expression of this power is forgiveness. I know, forgiveness may not sound all that powerful, but it is. Here are two reasons why.

First, forgiveness is the most radical antidote to the delusion of inequality, which is the enemy of humility. Our inequality-bathed world animates us with wicked energies, compelling us to exalt ourselves and to denigrate others. Insults, cut-downs, cheats, boasts, and lies surround us all—some of it passive, some of it overt, but all of it reinforcing hierarchy and inequality. But humility is an affirmation of equality. The humble know that reality is different than it appears. The world, however, does not know that yet. We are strangers in a foreign land, visitors to a primitive civilization. Everyone still operates as if inequality is reality. When we forgive, we echo Jesus's diagnosis of humanity, "They know not what they do" (Luke 23:34 ESV). Forgiveness is a signal that we understand the pervasiveness of this world's delusion. The apostle Paul, recognizing this mental illness of the world, advises us, "Be completely humble and gentle," and "be patient, bearing with one another in love" (Ephesians 4:2), just as you would treat someone you loved who was suffering from any other form of psychosis.

Second, forgiveness represents the ultimate expression of true freedom—for both senses of the word. The first sense of the word has to do with choice. Freedom of choice is far more evident when we make counterintuitive choices than when we go with the flow, do what we're supposed to do, or feel how we're supposed to feel.

And nothing is more counterintuitive, and *not* what you're supposed to do, than forgiving a debt, letting someone off the hook—without payment, without retribution, without justice. Forgiveness without retribution, or without confession even, is considered foolish in this world and is, therefore, an utmost expression of true freedom.

But forgiveness is also an ultimate expression of freedom in the other sense of the word. It is the ultimate liberation. When you forgive, you break a deep restraint. The people in our lives we leave unforgiven hold powerful places in our psyches. We burn through great personal resources just to hold them there. True, our psyches may need to hold them there for a while, but it's self-defeating in the long run.

Humbling yourself requires forgiveness because the unforgiven always remain oversized in our minds. Forgiveness always makes the perpetrator smaller, cuts them back down to size. "To forgive those who have wronged one is an act of highest sovereignty and great inner freedom," observes Moltmann, because forgiving topples the perpetrator's status in the victim's mind, freeing the victim from the "compulsion to evil deeds"—compulsion being the opposite of freedom.[12] Forgiveness demotes the violator, making them smaller, and redeems the violated, making them relatively bigger. In this way, forgiveness is a central tool in deconstructing inequality and in fostering equality.

Don't expect the voice inside of you, or your inner child, to coach you to forgive in these profound ways. Radical forgiveness like this only makes sense within the radical context from which Jesus calls us to humble ourselves. Only when you really believe in ultimate restoration can you forgo all futile attempts at retributive justice in the here-and-now. Only when we embrace the reality of equality and release all our demands for justice does such forgiveness make any sense. Only when you really believe the most important part of you is impervious to all violations can you wave these violations off by forgiving the debt.

When Jesus, at the climax of history's most extreme injustice, says, "Forgive them, Father," he is overthrowing vengeance, retributive justice, retaliation, and all other futile repayment philosophies. He is announcing *forgiveness* as the ultimate act of initiating restoration. "They know not what they do," Jesus says—they're delusional! As are those transfixed by the delusion of inequality around us. You might get angry at someone who knocks over the flower pots in your front yard. But when you discover she is schizophrenic and she thinks your flower pots are demons trying to break into your house, your anger toward her changes. That is, you would forgive her because she is clearly sick—she knows not what she does.

So too with those around us. We're all recovering, at various stages, from the delusion of inequality. Peter asks Jesus, "How many times should we forgive someone who sins against us? Seven?" Jesus replies, "seven times seventy" (Matthew 18:21–22), which is Jesus's way of telling Peter to forgive endlessly.

While inequality reigns, forgiveness must be persistent. In this way, Jesus promotes forgiveness as more of a mindset than a single act. Jesus wants us to breathe forgiveness. You are surrounded by false inequality; forgiveness reinforces the reality of equality. Transgressions, abuse, neglect, betrayal, lies, slander fall upon you in a torrential downpour—constant violations splattering against your face and heart, knocking over your flower pots. Forgiveness is your windshield wiper, set on high, swiping back and forth, tossing these endless infractions out of your path.

## GET ON THE ROAD!

Make no mistake, the humility Jesus unleashes is subversive and relentless. "Humble yourselves," Jesus says, which immediately nullifies an army of fruitless gurus and overthrows a thousand inept shepherds and their oppressive theologies-of-can't.

When we humble ourselves, we make God's love for us real in our lives by recognizing our profound security.

When we humble ourselves, we make equality real in our lives by disempowering shame and arrogance and steadfastly vanquishing all oppression.

When we humble ourselves, we take responsibility in our lives, vanquishing all powerlessness and passivity.

And finally, when we humble ourselves, we make our freedom real in our lives, most saliently expressed in our radical, habitual forgiveness of ourselves and others. Forgiveness and its offspring—tolerance, patience, and forbearance—are indicators that we are getting closer and closer to the humility Jesus teaches.

But humility does even more. It lays the foundation for authentic confidence.

# CHAPTER 7.

# THE ROAD TO CONFIDENCE

---

## WHAT CONFIDENCE IS

Growing in humility means growing into the truth that, deep inside, you are secure. Whether you acknowledge it or not, this security is yours, a gift bestowed upon you the moment you began to exist.

Confidence is different. We're not given confidence, it must be earned. Whereas security has to do with our innermost selves, confidence has to do with everything outside this core self—things like our skills and abilities, our looks, or our intelligence. Confidence is simply a type of trust. It's a personal assessment of how effective we believe ourselves to be at any given thing. The better I think I am at swimming, the more confident I am about swimming. The better I think I am at singing, the more confident I am about my voice.

We are secure. We can have confidence. Security is a gift. Confidence is an opportunity. Security is about our essence itself. Confidence is about what we do with that secure essence. Security says: "The world can't do anything inside me." Confidence says: "This is what I can do inside the world." Security is stable. Confidence fluctuates. Security is about what is *internal*—though it can be expressed externally. Confidence is about what is *external*—though it may be felt internally. The opposite of security is insecurity. The opposite of confidence is doubt, doubt about the effectiveness of a skill or asset.

We all want to be effective, so we all want confidence. We want it badly. A fascinating 2013 study, "Beauty Is in the Eye of the Beer Holder," found that people who were given juice but told that it was hard liquor rated themselves as more attractive, even though they merely thought they were drunk.[1] We want to be confident. We might even deceive ourselves to feel it—and some of us are even willing to take destructive chemicals to feel it.

## THE POWER OF CONFIDENCE

Confidence has been shown to be a potent force for contentment, effectiveness, and even healing. When you gain more control and increase your effectiveness at what you want to do, you are gaining power. Fear, anxiety, and depression are all symptoms of powerlessness. But getting good at something empowers us. It's why cancer patients experience less depression when they develop a new skill.[2] It's why "helplessness can be reversed and prevented by experience with success."[3] For people with eating disorders, new competencies lead to decreased emotional eating and increased resistance to social pressure to be thin.[4] For alcoholics, it improves control over alcohol consumption.[5]

There's no black magic here. You don't need to discover your inner guide. You don't need to go on a soul-journey. It's not the universe bending to your will. It's concrete and thoroughly attainable by anyone. We can all improve ourselves and master new skills. That is, we can all become more confident at the things we do.

## THE DITCHES SABOTAGE CONFIDENCE

The Ditch of Smallness has a hard time with confidence because confidence seems so blatantly pro-self—it's hard to be confident while also trying to despise yourself. Many try to live out their competency with a sort of resigned denial. With pursed lips and clenched fists, they fight to maintain their sense of smallness. They shrug off praise and smother any satisfaction that might swell within. And some of them must fight really hard because their competence is so great. Beautiful folks who claim to be ugly, intelligent people who play dumb, or, my favorite, the gifted athlete—say, the baseball pitcher who pitches a perfect game and when the television reporter asks him about the amazing accomplishment, the baseball player responds, "It's not me. It's all God."

As religious and spiritually grounded as this baseball player sounds, his statement is insincere.[6] Talking like this downplays the crucial role of skill development. It trivializes things like effort, perseverance, and self-correction. He leaves his listeners with the sense that success has nothing to do with what *you* do. Great forces far beyond your control are orchestrating the events of life for their own purposes. Good luck, and maybe those forces will bless you, too.

But confidence is not pride. You can be bursting with confidence without exhibiting even a trace of pride. Confidence, in fact, has little to do with you at all. To see this, say you and two rowdy friends are out tooling around on your boat and—oops—one of your friends, who can't swim, falls in, leaving only two of you in the boat. Which of you will be jumping in after your klutzy pal? Let's just say you happen to be a swim instructor, so you proclaim, "I'm the better swimmer! I'll go in after him!" Was it you who saved your friend, or was it your swimming ability? Obviously, it was merely your ability. And were you being arrogant by stating your superior ability? Of course not. But you were being confident.

The Ditch of Bigness warps confidence in a different way. Most people use the term *self-confidence* to refer simply to a person's entire set of skills and abilities. But Team Bigness seeks to puff the *self* up. Doped-up on self-esteem and positivity, Team Bigness globalizes confidence as having to do with the self-as-a-whole.

It's easy to spot. Trying to make the self, itself, confident, in this global way, comes off as vacuous, hot air that leads to little more than rah-rah noise and unjustified enthusiasm. It often involves motivational speakers, positive-thinking exercises, and pep-talks. But if I want to, say, be a computer programmer, no amount of peptalking will improve my confidence. I need to start learning a programming language. I need to start writing code. Everything else is noise.

## HUMILITY AND CONFIDENCE

Can you be confident and humble? Yes. In fact, humility is the only way to be truly confident. The reason comes back to the delusion of inequality and esteemating.

Esteemating is confidence poison. In the machine of esteemating, everything gets interpreted through self-worth calculation. Everything external to your essence (things like your skills, your looks, your personality, your heritage, and so forth) gets crammed into the calculator, the result of which is internalized, swallowed, plastered to the deepest part of yourself. This always leads to shame or pride—both of which kill confidence in that they agitate our focus. They exaggerate the importance of irrelevant things and they make us overly sensitive to outcomes.

I rolled my ankle about fifteen years ago (I won't tell you how, but it involved jogging, some cute ladies, and an unseen curb). The dumb ankle is still fragile now over a decade later! It gets reinjured easily. This fragility taints other areas of life. For instance, basketball. There was a time—oh, how sweet it was—when I played basketball with a free spirit and a total focus on my game. But after injuring my ankle, basketball has never been the same. I now devote a significant amount of attention to my ankle, monitoring my every action and step to keep myself from reinjuring it. This reduces my concentration on things like ball-handling, my shooting form, what my teammates are doing, or what the other team is doing on defense. My reflexes are delayed significantly as I assess for reinjury risk, and my overall basketball game is greatly diminished—and it wasn't that great to begin with.

Likewise, it's hard for us to live freely and naturally, to attend to the things we are doing in the way they need to be attended to, when we feel insecure. Insecurity takes priority over everything, whether we want it to or not. I want simply to focus on my basketball game, or my class presentation, but if I am insecure, the basketball game and the presentation get obscured. Security is the foundation of real confidence. Esteemating, by definition, betrays an insecure state.

Esteemating also adds extra meaning to everything, too. When someone esteemates, they are always trying to prove something about themselves. This extra objective gets added to the original goal. Such a person can't concentrate on the thing he is doing without the extra work of assessing all the potential threats and risks to his ego. This added bulk impairs everything he does. For instance, learning to play the violin somehow becomes *trying to be sufficient as a person by playing the violin.* Violin is no longer about the violin but about *them* and what mastery of the violin might say about them. This cognitive clutter is guaranteed to sabotage performance. When our security is tightly associated with our outcomes, every act, every performance, and every task can become an onerous danger to the self.

The antidote to all of this is humility.

As we grow in humility, we grow in trust that our worth is impenetrable—nothing we do can devalue it. Our sense of security was never meant to be bound to our performance, our skills, or our assets. The things we do were never meant to be indicators of worth. They mean nothing—not in any deep sense, anyway. And any idea that they do is delusional.

So, humbling yourself has much to do with unbinding your essence from everything external to that essence, and then reevaluating everything for what that thing is in itself. Humility means focusing on the violin only for the sake of playing the violin. It means focusing on your presentation about tree frogs only for the sake of sharing what you know about tree frogs.

Humility allows us to enjoy everything for what it is, not for what it says about us! And doesn't this make sense? Confidence for the sake of confidence is hollow.

We don't merely want to be confident about playing the violin, we actually want to make good music. We don't just want to be convinced that we are good singers, we actually want to be masters of our voice—maybe because we have songs we want to sing. What's most important to us, really, is competence. That's what we really want. In fact, confidence researcher Tomas Chamorro-Premuzic argues that low confidence can be far more beneficial to us than high confidence because we are more likely to try harder if we believe we are disadvantaged.[7] Although I don't think we should conjure feelings of low confidence, just as we should not pretend high confidence, his prioritization of competence over confidence is exactly right.

So, for the humble—for those not suffering under the delusion of inequality—the outcome of any given performance has little relevance to, and no effect on, our security. Our sense of self is stable, immune to the fluctuations of health, wit, or accomplishment. And as we come to really see this, to really believe it, a great deal of anxiety dissipates, leaving us with far more mental space for things like concentration, creative responsiveness, and emotion regulation. This in turn helps us perform better, and a better performance will thereby increase our confidence all the more.

This idea, that performance is irrelevant, has another advantage. If we really are invulnerable to all these external things, then we can also look at our failures openly and without apprehension. In day-to-day life, we no longer have the need to deny weaknesses or hide vulnerabilities. And she who can fearlessly face her weaknesses will have a far easier time overcoming them than she who denies them.

Related to this, the irrelevance of performance allows

us to affirm our strengths without fear of arrogance. We can say "I am a great cook" without pomp, because we know being a great cook does not matter in any deep sense. We can have pride in our PhD dissertation without being a proud self—without condescension or haughtiness.

## WHAT CONFIDENCE IS NOT

### CONFIDENCE IS NOT MERELY A FEELING

The biggest mistake people make is they try to feel confident. They listen to pep-talks and go to motivational speakers, hoping to get charged up. They look for quotes to inspire them and chase down all sorts of strange cognitive tricks hoping to stoke some inner feeling of confidence. Pep-talks and motivational speeches can generate gads of enthusiasm—enough to fill a stadium—but not a shred of actual confidence.

Confidence is a different type of cognition altogether. Confidence calculates, makes judgments, appraises skills and assets—all cognitions that take place in various sections of the cortex. Confidence needs evidence. We need to see success. We need to actually be good at a skill, or excel at some attribute, and be able to verify it through our senses. When we do, we grow in confidence—which, of course, can then lead to a variety of pleasant feelings that are triggered deeper in the brain, in the limbic system, the amygdala, and the hippocampus. We first perform actions of competence, then experience feelings of confidence.

## CONFIDENCE IS NOT OPTIMISM

Some people consider confidence as a sort of attitude—particularly, a positive attitude. But confidence does not arise out of optimism or positive thinking. Confidence emerges from cold, dispassionate evaluation—the result of which can *cause* positive attitudes but is not positive or negative in itself.

## CONFIDENCE IS NOT REQUIRED

You don't need it. Really! Because you are secure, it doesn't really matter how much confidence you have. Confidence sits before you as an opportunity. It's there for the taking, and it can make your life a great deal better. But it can't make your self better. Confidence is wonderful, but also, in a way, not that big of a deal.

## BARRIERS TO CONFIDENCE

### PERFECTIONISM

Perfectionism is born out of insecurity, not security. Perfectionism is, in fact, lazy—a lazy reaction to the pressures and stresses of esteemating. It's a symptom of a person trapped tightly in the clutches of the delusion of inequality. When we esteemate, so much is at stake. We must maintain our high scores, our elite status, and keep our egos safe from the burning pits of shame. So, we try to dominate the esteemating game by scoring perfectly on everything. We try to secure ourselves on the desired side of the esteemating equation by dominating all of our important external attributes.

We all want to perform the best we can. We want excellence, and that's healthy. But perfectionism is unhealthy.

Perfectionism establishes a corrosive binary in our mind, an unhelpful disjunct, convincing us that perfection is the only valuable result. Perfectionists care too much. Their anxiety swells beyond normal performance anxiety. There's little peace in there, and satisfaction is rare.

"Winning isn't everything, it's the only thing," Vince Lombardi said, in his toxic sermon to perfectionists everywhere. But winning isn't the only thing. With the humble, peace is constant. Failure cannot hurt us, it can only help us.

## POSITIVE THINKING

Authentic confidence is a calculation that must be justified. It requires accuracy. The more accurate and well-founded our assessments are, the stronger our confidence will be in the long run. In this way, confidence just so happens to require negative thinking. To become more competent, which is the source of confidence, a critical mind is essential. We need to know our weaknesses. We need to know our flaws.

When it comes to your essence, a critical voice is a terrible nemesis. But when it comes to competence, the critical voice is often the hero. The critical voice diagnoses our weakness, so we can begin working on a treatment plan. This is why negative thoughts are natural to us. We use critical thought to protect ourselves, to detect dangers and risks, and to discover where we can improve. Critical thinking doesn't work without the critical part. People are apprehensive about critical thinking, and negative thoughts, because they can often devolve into painful *self*-criticism. But when we understand the reality of equality and the stability of our worth, these normal and natural self-criticisms are not a threat. In fact, they are valuable.

| Esteemating | Humble Confidence |
|---|---|
| Winning is everything | Winning is nice but not everything |
| Losing is bad | Losing can be good |

## OVERCONFIDENCE

We've all been duped by overconfidence. Who hasn't set a goal to save money or lose weight, only to find their wealth making no gain and their weight making no loss?[8] Inflated expectations come easily for us, in part because we're such capable creatures. Think of all you've mastered just to become an adult. You've conquered communication, mobility, time management, abstract thought, and so much more. You're amazing! So, for good reason, your expectations inflate, to an extent, all on their own.

When we mix in the steroids of self-esteem and positive thinking, the inflation of expectation can quickly get out of control, leading to chronic overconfidence—"an unrealistic belief in one's ability to succeed."[9] We assume we can when maybe we shouldn't, we expect success when success is unlikely, and we press on and persist in endeavors that are doomed to fail. When we only consider the positives, we convince ourselves that we will succeed, no matter how solid the evidence to the contrary may be.

Optimal effectiveness at anything requires concentration, attention, and maximum effort. But these are exactly the types of things you don't find in a person who is overconfident. Perry notes, "People engage in greater processing activity when they feel doubtful," not when they feel positive.[10] Confidence without justification, without evidence, *is* overconfidence and does us little good. In fact, it's not really even confidence at all. It's just empty hope.

## UNDER-CONFIDENCE

It's true that low confidence can be beneficial in learning a new skill. Realizing you are not where you want to be in that skill provides the framework necessary for you to move forward. You won't invest the focus and energy necessary to get to where you want to be if you think you're already there. But even then, it's not low confidence itself that's the hero. Rather, it's the appraisal undergirding the low confidence that benefits you. If you appraise your skill as effective, thereby leading to confidence, great! If you appraise your skill and conclude it to be deficient, thereby triggering low confidence, that can be great, too! What's not helpful is having low confidence not based on any actual assessment.

The Ditch of Smallness contributes to this brand of free-floating low confidence, both directly and indirectly. Directly, the mandate to repel all pride, to renounce all self-praise, stifles our self-appraisals, filling our expectations with unnecessary gravity. Indirectly, the Ditch of Smallness encourages low confidence with one of its primary principles: self-focus is bad. But self-focus is not bad. In fact, confidence requires an amount of self-focus. It requires you to monitor your skills, to check your results, to regulate your emotions, and a whole litany of self-administrative tasks as you steer your complicated self to greater and greater efficacy and competence. How much time you spend thinking of yourself is not the issue. The point is, if you want to master a skill, you must be thinking about yourself.

Team Smallness often recoils at the threat of self-focus, but the irony is, avoiding self-focus often prolongs self-focus. The path to self-forgetfulness, which Team Smallness wants, is competence, not self-abnegation. The more proficient you become, the less you have to think about yourself! Basketball again provides a good analogy. When you're first starting out, you need to think a great deal about your shooting form. But elite shooters will tell you that once you gain a certain level of mastery, thinking about your mechanics actually sabotages performance. Good shooters don't calculate how hard they have to throw the ball and at what angle. Rather, they look at the hoop and trust their practiced self to figure all that out for them.

## INCREASING CONFIDENCE

### PURSUE EXCELLENCE

With humble confidence we seek excellence, not personal perfection. Excellence is about my performance, perfectionism is about me. When we pursue excellence, we try to perform perfectly. When we are mesmerized in a fit of perfectionism, we are trying to be perfect based on our performance. That is, we are trying to gain security from the outside in. Perfectionism is a pathological, impossible pursuit. It turns people off. Excellence is exhilarating and inspiring. It draws people in.

### DO STUFF

Confidence grows based on evidence. Confidence will never grow if we don't do anything. Sitting around thinking about music theory will not improve our confidence. We must actually hit the keys and pluck the strings.

For the insecure, where the fear of poor performance is a terrible threat to self-worth, starting can be difficult. But humble confidence is secure and therefore not afraid of terrible performance. In fact, to the humble, a terrible performance can be a fantastic start to our journey! Jesus's humble followers don't assume they can or can't. Rather, they act. Then they assess. Then they act again.

## DON'T CONFUSE COMPETITION AND CONFLICT

They are not the same thing. Competition is about who is more skillful at accomplishing some arbitrary objective. Conflict is about who is right about some substantial disagreement. Competition seeks to accentuate differences. Conflict seeks to resolve differences. In competition, the goal is to win. In conflict, trying to win is a terrible goal that simply escalates the conflict. In a conflict, the goal is resolution. In competition, resolution is ridiculous.

| Competition | Conflict |
|---|---|
| Trying to Win: GOOD | Trying to Win: BAD |
| Seeking Resolution: BAD | Seeking Resolution: GOOD |

The delusion of inequality converts every competition into a conflict and every conflict into a competition. If my performance can deplete me in some deep, inner way, then you will injure me if you win. The fun, free-spirited nature of competition, the arbitrariness of the objective, is lost within the fog of esteemating. When we're trapped in the carnival of self-worth calculation, there are no arbitrary objectives. Everything could hurt us. But within the security of humility, we can now look at another's victory or success with peace, and even joy, because we know the boundaries of its meaning.

## A CONFIDENT TRAVELER

Becoming confident first requires growing in humility, pushing back against esteemating and the delusion of inequality. It then requires detaching everything—accomplishments, skills, or personal assets—from your essence and evaluating them for what they are, on their own merits, apart from what they say about you. As we learn new skills and engage the world in new ways, we must retrain our emotions according to this new framework. Maybe we're used to feeling dread about an upcoming performance. We must wrestle out of this dread, as we now know there really isn't much at stake. We may be used to frustration at failure. We must now learn to curtail these frustrations, as we now know that failure can't hurt us, it can only help us.

It helps me to think of life as a hospital. We will soon see the doctor and he will assess our health. But most of our time spent here is in the waiting room. We read magazines. We throw paper balls at the wastebasket. We pass the time until we can see who we came to see. The world, instead of helping us prepare for our examination, tries to convince us that the waiting room itself is the reason we are here and is itself the most important thing. But I agree with C. S. Lewis, who considered most things "raw material," with no inherent value. Humility has much to do with recognizing this inherent neutrality in things and engaging them accordingly.

Confident humility recognizes that we are invincible

where it matters most and vulnerable only in arbitrary things. In this way, much of what the world considers threatening really isn't. We don't have to be so pent up. We don't have to be so defensive. As the toil of esteemating falls away, leaving us in the relaxed magic of humility, work transforms into play. As we disentangle from the false and hostile world of inequality, the real and secure world opens up to us as a playground, a playground overflowing with opportunity for adventure. Of course, we don't have to do anything here, but we can. And as we experience the peace and vitality that emerges from greater humility and confidence, we want to.

# CHAPTER 8.

# THE ROAD TO SOCIAL VITALITY

---

Jesus calls us to a radical revolution of self, which leads to a profound revolution of relationship and community. To see this, I must first unpack an important truth. Almost all mental health and spiritual health is relational.

## PSYCHOLOGY IS SOCIAL

What if you were the last person on earth? Say you wake one morning alone in the world, with no cars on the streets, no planes in the skies, and no personalities cackling on social media. Nobody. Anywhere. Where did they go? You don't know. Maybe they were abducted by aliens. Maybe they were raptured.

You'd have many questions, certainly. For our purposes, I want you to ask this: How would it change the way you view yourself? Think about this honestly. Would you fix your hair each morning? Would you suck in your gut throughout the day? Would you feel as much anxiety about that big zit on your face? You wouldn't care about such things, would you? I bet you wouldn't even give them a second thought. "Nobody would be there to see," you'd say, and you'd be right. Really, all of our weaknesses and flaws, which pester us in this world of others, wouldn't bother us much at all. Psychology is social. Shame and pride, esteeming and humility, are all socially indexed. They have to do with how we view others and how we think others view us.

Even self-worth is relational. In a world of others, we want to be accepted, and this acceptance is the primary currency of self-worth. When I ask if I am worthy, what I'm really asking is whether I am acceptable to others.

## NOT JUST ANY LOVE WILL DO

But what do we mean by *acceptance*? It means that others consider us important, and they include us in their lives. We want to be okay to them, and we want them to value us and to have good thoughts about us. Things like that. We want to be loved.

But that word, *love*, is so worn out. Everyone overuses it—from hippies to politicians, from advertisers to pop musicians. Plus, the word has more applications than an iPhone. We love our dog. We love our pals. We love cookies. We love God. We love our country. We love our spouse. We love root beer.

But do we really feel the same for root beer as we do for our spouse?

Of course not.

Being loved stabilizes us with a force greater than anything else we can experience, but not just any love. The ancient Greeks understood this. They had four different words to represent different types of love. You have *storge* for your dog, *phileo* for your friends, and *eros* for your spouse. Each type of love with its own nuanced word. A place for everything, and everything in its place.

But then there is one more type of love, the greatest of them all. *Agape*.

For all the talk in our society about the importance of love, what gets promoted is not agape, but often an amalgamation of *storge, phileo*, and *eros*. Yet when we examine these other loves closely, and really get at the core of what these loves are all about, we end up with something quite different than agape. Society gets the diagnosis right: humanity needs love. But we screw up the prescription and think any love will do.

It doesn't take long to see the key differences. The first three loves have two features in common. First, they are each reactionary. We become affectionate in response to a cute dog (*storge*)—it just happens. We enjoy the company of certain friends (*phileo*)—we just click. And, finally, we are aroused by our significant other (*eros*)—we get turned on. Second, they are each marked by an emotional experience. Fluffy dogs make us feel good. Laughing with friends can be exhilarating. An encounter with a romantic partner can leave us euphoric. Thus, each love is experienced wholly within ourselves to the extent that, to grow in these types of love, we must experience more of these internal states. These loves are each emotion-based and reactive. They happen *to* us, in various degrees.[1]

Agape is the opposite. It's neither reactionary nor compelled by emotion. Agape is proactive. We choose it. It exists because we call it into existence, not as an automatic reaction or as the result of circumstantial correlation. In fact, we may not even really like the person we have chosen to agape. And since it exists purely from my choice, and not on the merits of the other, it is the purest of all loves.

Agape can result in emotions but is fundamentally

emotionless. It does not swell and deflate like emotional loves always do. Agape is not sentimental. In fact, it has very little to do with our inner experiences at all. Rather, when we have agape for another it's for the sake of that other. Thus, agape is an other-oriented love.

The truth is, *storge* will never fulfill us. It will never meet our deepest need for acceptance. *Phileo* without agape is fickle. Friends change, their interests change, we may lose common ground with them, we may no longer enjoy their company. *Eros* without agape is oh-so fragile. Sometimes feelings fade, physical attraction dissipates, and sometimes one partner becomes attracted to someone else. These oft-promoted loves are, at their core, unstable and transient.

But agape is not contingent on feelings or based on personal benefit. Agape is not "doing what makes you feel good, it's doing what is good despite how you feel."[2] It can be trusted to endure. It abides in our lives with the stability and predictability of the spinning earth.

I'm not being naïve. People betray us, including people we have agape love for. This danger is sewn into us. We are free. Even Jesus—who walked on water, healed the sick, raised the dead, and died for the sins of humanity—was betrayed by Judas. So of course, we can still be betrayed. Agape is still risky—in fact, since we do it regardless of personal benefit, it's probably the riskiest of all loves. But Jesus calls us to it anyway. Even betrayal does not invalidate agape. Nor does a betrayal from one agape lover inauthenticate our other agape relationships. Betrayal simply reveals that God has given us real freedom, even freedom to sabotage agape. Jesus calls us to agape love despite the risk, and the purity of agape love will both strengthen the willing and weed out the unwilling.

## AGAPE COMMUNITY

That so much of mental health is relational points us to a vital truth. We were made, from the inside out, to connect with others. This is why, when a whole community demonstrates agape, special things happen. Look at Jesus's prayer in John 17:20–26. Here, Jesus prays on our behalf that we might have the same love for one another that exists within God himself (agape), and that, through this love, we humans "may be one just as we [the Trinity] are one." When agape forms the structure of a community, that community reflects God himself. In other words, when we enter into agape love relationship, we enter into the very nature of God. When we agape, we participate in the very same baffling power that unifies the Trinity. "God didn't intend to be glorified primarily by individuals," notes Greg Boyd. God is, rather, "a social, triune God, and thus he created a world in which everything humans do works effectively only when it is done in relationships."[3] Agape is the foundation of everything God is trying to accomplish.

Humans are never told that we can share in God's omnipotence, nor can we cogitate with God's omniscience. We can, however, live and dwell in the richness of his agape. So, when we enter into agape relationships, transcendent things happen, the finite experiences the infinite, the limited connects to the unlimited.

The kingdom of God is first about being in agape community, more so even than having the right theology, or even being holy. Like me, Larry Crabb believes that God has placed "extraordinary resources within us that have the power to heal us,"[4] and "something wonderful and beautiful and resilient is within us that no abuse, rejection, or failure can ever destroy."[5] This healing power is ignited through the nourishment of agape bonds. "Let me put it plainly," says Crabb, "the center of a forgiven person is not sin [Ditch of Smallness]. Neither is it psychological complexity [Ditch of Bigness]. The center of a person is the capacity to connect."[6] Agape *is* this connection. For this reason, I believe we find in agape love, and only in agape love, the greatest power for radical personal change.

From brain to bone, we are made to live in rich agape fellowship, where each of us lives with committed, other-oriented hearts. The more we grow into this life, the more things happen inside of us. Powerful forces both within us and between us are ignited, creating a sense of unity that strengthens and nourishes each of us in ways that nothing else can. Agape love unleashes the very life of God within, which can heal us and bring us enduring contentment in the face of any circumstance. Because we are made for this, we long for it and desire it, and when we do not have it, we substitute cheap imitations.

In agape community, we each play a key role, and the community becomes part of our individual identities. The *us* infiltrates the *me*—but not so much that my sense of personal identity dissolves into the group. I don't lose myself. Rather, my individuality becomes supercharged and expands as it connects to the power grid that is agape community. The whole is greater than the sum of its parts, but the parts are also each greater when connected properly to the whole. The more we build up agape community the more agape community builds us up.

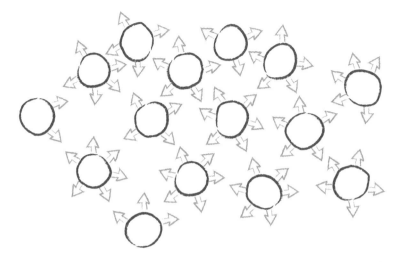

Agape community where each member lives with other-oriented, choice-based love for one another.

As our roots grow deeper and deeper into agape community, what the apostle Paul refers to as "the body of Christ" (1 Corinthians 12:27), we become increasingly secure and empowered—so much so that we find ourselves more and more willing to make greater and greater self-sacrifices for the benefit of others. Luke boasts about those in the early church selling their possessions and sharing everything in common (Acts 2:44). In fact, some of these same people ultimately gave their lives for the body. The bonds of agape love can become so strong they become worthy of self-sacrifice, maybe even ultimate self-sacrifice.

To be clear, selling everything we own is not the place to start our agape journey. We are not called to be naïve. And nobody is killing themselves to prove their love or any nonsense like that. The point is to demonstrate the real potential that agape can have in community. It can become so pure that we share all we have, including our very lives. The New Testament authors gave us a peek at the radical things mature agape love will do in us. They did not mean that doing radical things is the pathway to mature agape community.

## CONTRACT SOCIETY

I know, I know, this all sounds like weirdo utopian propaganda. It sounds like a land of unicorns and double rainbows. "Life is nothing like this," you may be thinking, and you're right. It isn't. The world we live in is fundamentally and thoroughly opposite of agape community. What we live in might better be described as a contract society.

Contract society is a hot, sad struggle compared to agape society. In contract society, relationships are primarily established based on personal benefit. "What do I get out of it?" Contract society is the land of terms and conditions and prenuptial agreements. It's the land of self-orientation—heck, self-obsession—where we learn a peculiar brand of love, a reactive, emotional, and self-serving love that may very well elate us, but can never fulfill us.

Of course, even in agape community, we all have preferences. We want our friends to have certain characteristics. We look for certain things in a spouse. Having preferences and criteria is normal. But in a contract society, the criteria are the whole show—it's all there is. "Don't waste time with people who don't add value to your life," gurus will advise, because that's what contract society is all about.

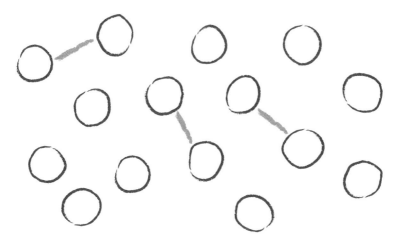

*In a contract society, each member lives in self-oriented competition with the other members.*

Contract society is a fragile mishmash of transient bonds, where our place is never secure unless we are always adding value. Our relationships are only as enduring as the benefits each member receives, but as soon as the relationship no longer pays dividends to either party, it is quickly discarded. In a contract society, we're always assessing and always being assessed. We're always evaluating the payoff of every relationship, of every interaction. Functionally, we are judges. Fundamentally, we are alone.

Of course, agape love is possible within this cold, strange place, otherwise Jesus would not have called us to it. But it's not natural. It's not the default. This world erects a wide variety of obstacles to agape. An unholy practicality motivates life in the contract world, a practicality that is always aware of life's limitations (money, time, land, resources, and so forth). We are born into this all-encompassing system of self-centeredness, which hums deep and inconspicuous, making it so easy to march along, totally oblivious to its melodies. Little-by-little, beneath our awareness, we give in, increasingly becoming self-centered cogs in the big, alluring, loveless machine of contract society.

Deep inside we know it's not what we are made for. We feel out of place. It's as if we are each a puzzle piece somehow placed in the wrong puzzle. Until we discover where we really belong, and how we really fit, we will forever find ourselves bent and jammed as we try to force ourselves into places we were not made for. "The problem beneath our struggles," says Crabb, "is a disconnected soul." We belong in agape community, and the more we are able to connect in agape love, the more we are able to tap into the most powerful force of change available to us. Those who fail to connect wander in various states of frantic insecurity, a state that Jesus called "harassed and helpless" (Matthew 9:36).

## HUMILITY RESTORES AGAPE COMMUNITY

We're all fogged over by the delusion of inequality, and contract society is the natural result. Others are seen not as brothers and sisters but as benchmarks against which we measure our own position—or worse, stepping stones upon which we leverage ourselves higher. Other people become opportunities and liabilities, to cling to or to avoid, for our own benefit and potential.

To visualize this, take the contract society graphic and turn it on its side:

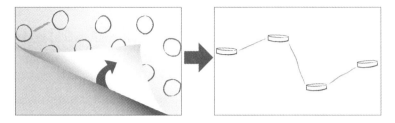

*Side view of contract society, showing its built-in hierarchical structure.*

You may feel like you are doing well, getting ahead, and going places in the contract society—and maybe you are! After all, we are adaptive creatures. We figure out how to succeed in all circumstances, including inequality. But the more effective we become at inequality, at living within contract society, the more incompatible we become with agape community. The two communities require different skills and different types of people, just as the better a person becomes at sumo wrestling, the less ideal they become for competitive swimming. Inequality simply doesn't work with agape.

Furthermore, even when things are going well in a contract society, shame roars nearby. We can't rest. We can't take our eye off the prize. We must always be adding value, always growing profits, always conquering bigger mountains. Success can feel good, but the goodness is always temporary and tempered. We know that any wrong move—saying the wrong thing, doing something stupid—can send our value into a tailspin, leaving us dizzy in our self-contempt. Contract society is exhausting. It's like riding on a fragile, homemade Ferris wheel. It goes up and down in a tedious cycle of dread and relief, and most people don't even know they can get off the ride.

They can.

Humility establishes the structure that makes real connection—agape relationship—possible. When we are properly oriented to others in humility, the goodness of agape can flow into us and out of us the way it is supposed to. When we reject inequality and accept equality, and when we acknowledge the worth of each person, and therefore our own worth, the gears inside of us align. The teeth fall into the grooves, and things begin humming inside us the way they're supposed to. Agape is the magic, humility is the structure the magic flows through.

Becoming compatible with agape society means letting go of the habits and tactics of contract society—as effective as those tactics might have been in this sad arena—and developing the habits and tactics of agape love. It's a long way from here to there. But the first step is the most important. Reject the delusion of inequality and embrace humility. Turn from self-worth calculation and lean on the abundant security we already have. As all of us embrace the truth of equality, and as we all grow in agape, the fundamental structure of society changes:

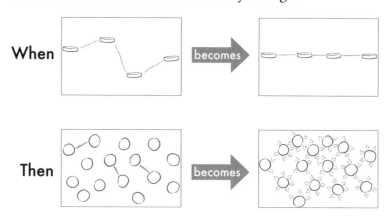

*When we change how we evaluate one another, society itself can change.*

We can now sincerely "put on love" for one another, which binds "all together in perfect unity" (Colossians 3:14—note the choice-based, proactive language of *putting on love*). As the gears of humility first come together within us, as the machine starts revving and humming, previously dormant powers begin churning. Everything feels different.

This isn't just grandiose talk. It's level-headed, thoroughly rational good news. We've already seen how humility undermines perfectionism, disempowers shame and pride, and makes authentic confidence possible. But it does even more. It's when humility bombinates within us that we are the most teachable and the most correctable. When we are self-loathing, any rebuke we receive gets misdirected. "This is what you did wrong" gets translated into "this is further evidence of your worthlessness," which we can't do anything with. Meanwhile, those stoned on self-esteem struggle to take the very need for correction seriously. They scoff and minimize and shrug everything down to size and remain blissfully ignorant of their flaws.[7] But in the fertile sphere of humility, our ears are clear, and rebuke and correction are power pellets we devour. We assume we're not perfect, that we have much to learn, so we have incentive to listen. Yet we also know we are capable of learning and improving, so we forgo self-loathing and take action. We power-up on the guidance of the wise, with no thought to our egos, so we can be nourished and made more effective. "Let the righteous person smite me," the psalmist says, "let him rebuke me—that is kindness; that is oil on my head" (Psalm 141:5, author's paraphrase).

"The greatest in the kingdom is the one who serves," Jesus says, and yanks the power cord out of self-obsession. He fully affirms our ability to achieve but orients that ability in a way that destroys all inclinations for self-obsession. In fact, Jesus challenges us to perfection! In the Sermon on the Mount, Jesus commands us to "be perfect, therefore, as your heavenly father is perfect" (Matthew 5:48). But this is not the cheap perfection that we've been familiarized with in our world of inequality. In a contract society, perfection is all about the flowering of the self. It's about having the lowest body fat, the quickest wit, the right style, successful acquaintances, and so forth. But Jesus commands something far more robust.

The key word in his command is "therefore," which indicates that his call to perfection is the conclusion to a larger message. We see that message in Matthew 5:1–48, where Jesus expounds on how we should treat each other, how we should stay loyal, how we should treat those we hate, and how we should carry out justice. In other words, perfection is about how we participate in effective agape community. The perfection Jesus calls us to is measured by how effective our relationships are, how strong our communities are, and whether the underprivileged are taken care of. Being perfect by this measure might even *diminish* individual achievement![8]

## CONNECTING

### LOVE OTHERS

Let me tell you a secret. We were made for agape love, so we are nourished by it even if it is not reciprocated. We don't have to wonder if people will love us back. When we agape love someone, that outgoing love blooms inside of us in a way that can be satisfying, fulfilling, and energizing all by itself.

That our outgoing love can enrich us may seem strange to some. Contract society, with its pragmatic "what do I get out of it" mindset, deadens our sensitivity to the protein of outgoing love. When we only love those who reciprocate love, we get no practice, no experience, with pure, concentrated, outgoing love. But the more we love those who cannot love us back, the more sensitive and perceptive we become to the secret nourishment hidden in our outgoing love.

When we gain the knack of detecting and absorbing the nourishment of outgoing love, we gain a special power. We gain an indestructible independence, one that cannot be crushed by any oppressor, human or otherwise. Helping people tap into this, into the sustenance of outgoing love, can be as healing as being loved. When we tap into the power of our own outgoing love, and when we see the impact our love has on others, we gain evidence of our power. That is, we become empowered. It's no surprise, then, that serving others has been shown to be effective at combating depression and anxiety. Plus, it helps to shift our hot spotlight off ourselves, if for only a short while.

So, we work to love everyone, out of choice, without expectation of reciprocation. But it's tough. It's work. Some people are difficult to love. They fill our lives with only nastiness and bad vibes. The work of love is treating people as they really are (vessels of infinite worth) despite how they behave, what they look like, or what they say. As Bruxy Cavey puts it, "Love is the will to work for the honor of a person," even when that person may not seem so honorable to us.[9] This requires all the fruits of humility, including tolerance. We assume they're trying their best with the circumstances they've been given. And if that's not true, we assume they've been hurt, misled, or are a slave to more powerful forces, like addiction, mental illness, or debt. Agape love simply means we "believe the good that exists deep within every regenerate heart is potentially stronger than all the bad that is there," and we "identify, nourish, and release the life of God in others by connecting with them."[10] The opportunity for agape love comes in finding that lovable essence of the other, which exists somewhere in there, though it might need to be excavated, brushed off, and exposed to the light.

## LOVE YOURSELF

We can't really love others if we don't love ourselves. Or, as Jesus said it, "love your neighbor as yourself" (Matthew 22:39). This means our love for others is self-indexed. Given what we've discovered about our fundamental equality, this should make sense. Jesus tells us that we are all equal, so my appraisal of you can't be better or worse than my appraisal of myself.

The Ditch of Smallness fails at this. "I am a despicable wretch, a worthless speck—oh, but you're great!" This doesn't work. Even praise, when it comes from someone wallowing in self-contempt, rings hollow. There's a floor to how lowly we can view ourselves and still connect with others meaningfully.

Of course, we can't really love others if we exalt ourselves, either. Narcissists have a hard time connecting with anyone—other than dependent personalities—because they bring an agenda to every relationship. They view every interaction for what it says about them. Even when they're serving others, it's often just a photo op to show how benevolent they are.

## ALLOW OTHERS TO LOVE YOU

Be served. We all know God values servitude, charity, and general orientation toward others. But esteemating can hijack even these core kingdom gestures. We get wrapped up in giving and serving and tally up those acts as points toward being a great Christian, and the thought of someone serving us can feel like an affront to our holy project. Or, the idea of someone providing for us makes us feel needy and somehow beneath them, so we are averse to gifts.

During college I worked as a waiter, and believe me, people have a hard time letting other people buy them food. I've seen conversations about who is going to pay a dinner check devolve into heated, nasty arguments. We get so entangled in our own false holiness that we can't even allow someone to buy us ravioli and bread sticks!

Even though our outgoing love of others can really nourish us, it's God's intent that we should also experience agape from others. Watch for this in Jesus. We see him modeling both giving love and receiving love. Even Jesus, who emptied himself of his divinity, took on our constraints, died for us, and washed our feet—even he allowed others to serve him. He graciously defended the woman who anointed his feet. He reclined at the dinner table in the upper room and ate the big meal prepared for him. Jesus served others and allowed others to serve him.

God wants us to be servants—all of us. But we can't all be servants if nobody is served. "It is difficult to accept all the time," said Joy Gresham, after cancer debilitated her, "but unless we did, how could others have the pleasure, and the spiritual growth, of giving?"[11] But we struggle with accepting service. Why? I believe it's pride—a pride that those in the Ditch of Smallness, ironically, are most guilty of. They fixate on an image of martyring themselves, and belittling themselves, and putting themselves below others, and they imagine, I presume, the praise that will fall upon them for their meekness. But none of this is the goal of servitude. Joy Gresham, again, captures this well. "I don't know about you, but I was very proud; I liked the superior feeling of helping others, and for me it is much harder to receive than to give but, I think, much more blessed."

## CONCLUSION

God commands us to be humble because humility reflects reality and is the necessary precondition for becoming agape lovers. We were made to be agape lovers, which is why agape love nourishes our spirit like nothing else can. As agape love grows, so does the reality of unity. "It is the essence of love," says Bonhoeffer, "that it should lie beyond all disunion."[12] The magnetism of this unity is agape love. Within the unifying bonds of agape love, all arbitrary differences dissolve, to the extent that "there is neither Jew nor Gentile, neither slave nor free, nor is there male and female, for you are all one in Christ Jesus" (Galatians 3:28).

Becoming humble agape lovers involves pulling back the curtain to discover the hidden forces that have been harassing and bullying us with shame and arrogance. It means accepting the peculiar narrative Jesus calls us to, that we are all "brothers and sisters." Jesus calls us to this not because he wants us to be peculiar but because this is true reality. It represents how things really are, despite appearances.

Growing into this reality requires acclimating to the truth that you have unsurpassable worth, established by God's love for you. This means learning to let go of whatever frantic methods you previously used to secure your worth. You don't have to earn anything. You don't have to do anything. Security is yours. But you can do things. God filled the world with toys and games and adventures. As you grow into the security of humility, you can go out and play. And since your worth is invulnerable, you now do things because you want to. Instead of being forced into the playground by your need to prove yourself, now you can be drawn into the world by the joy of its toys.

# CHAPTER 9.

# A HUMBLE TRAVELER

In the movie *A Beautiful Mind*, the 2001 masterpiece about Nobel Prize–winning economist John Nash, Nash out-smarts his mental illness. As a schizophrenic, Nash had persistent, ongoing hallucinations (interacting with people who were not really there) and false beliefs (he was the target of global conspiracy). All Nash wanted to do in life, his great passion, was math. But the disruptive grandios-ity of his schizophrenia made doing math impossible. He tried medication, which tempered his psychosis, but the brutal side effects made math impossible in a different way. He was trapped. His only hope, if he wanted to do math again, would be to outsmart his illness. So, he began developing tactics to test his experiences to determine if they were real or not. In the movie, for instance, he con-cluded that one of his long-term friends, a little girl, was not real because, "She never ages."

Jesus tells us we are also in a delusional state, and reality is not what it seems. Humility reflects reality, but it is cloaked and obscured within the lies of the contract soci-ety, within the fog of the delusion of inequality, and under the heavy weight of esteemating. Becoming humble means deconstructing thick falsehoods and uncovering complicated lies. It means learning to see past an intricate facade that deceives us, distracts us, and traps us.

Our work is much like the work Nash did. We need tactics to test our experiences, to help us work ourselves out of esteemating and inequality and to get us onto the solid ground of humility. In this practical, boots-to-the-ground section, I want to present five such tactics.

## TRAVEL TACTIC ONE: TELL THE TRUTH IN DETAIL

There's a saying I've always liked. "We make choices, then our choices make us." The aphorism punctuates the cumulative importance of choice, and that's what I like about it—because it's easy for us to take our choices for granted. If each choice feeds into who we will become, then each choice is momentous. There's meaning in every step. The Bible also emphasizes this importance of choice. "I have set before you life and death," God says, "choose life" (Deuteronomy 30:19). Each choice is a life-or-death moment. The apocryphal text Sirach makes this choice more concrete and vivid, saying God has "placed before you fire and water; you can stretch out your hand for whichever you choose" (Sirach 15:16).

It seems like a no-brainer. Of course we'll choose water, right? And yet, so often we choose fire. We want water—we are so very thirsty—but the distortion fields of the ditches and the delusion of inequality make it hard to see straight. We find ourselves standing in this strange dystopian world where the fire so often looks just like the water.

The ditches contribute to this. They nudge us from reality—the reality of who we are—and they distort the nature of God's love for us. They pry us toward global falsehoods: "You are fundamentally good," or, "You are fundamentally bad." The more we think and act within these false perspectives the more these falsehoods accumulate, until, as John says, "We deceive ourselves and the truth is not in us" (1 John 1:8). When this happens, we lose control, or, as Paul says, "I do not do the good I want to do, but the evil I do not want to do" (Romans 7:19).

What can we do? How can we work ourselves out of falsehood? How can we make water look like water again, and fire look like fire?

The answer is confession, a habitual, consistent, effective lifestyle of truthful confession—to yourself, to God, and to others. James tells us: "Confess your sins . . . that you may be healed" (James 5:16). Truthful confession heals (or keeps us from getting hurt in the first place). David says, "When I refused to confess my sin, my body wasted away, and I groaned all day long" (Psalm 32:3, New Living Translation). Confession pushes back against the lies inside. It's the first step in wrestling back control over our lives.

But it's tricky. Even confession has been abducted by the ditches. The Ditch of Bigness makes confession superfluous. When you are good enough just the way you are, there is nothing to confess. Plus, when you are avoiding everything negative, chances are you won't give much consideration to sin. Prayer, in the Ditch of Bigness, is often full of praise and gratitude. Praise and gratitude are wonderful! But they are not confession. We are in a war for our spirits. Lies encroach upon us from every side. We need to develop skill at seeing ourselves for what we really are. We need to develop skill at speaking truth. We need confession.

The Ditch of Smallness sabotages confession in a different way. If you believe you are wholly bad, sinful behaviors are expected. They're self-explanatory. When you sin, you are simply being your sinful self. You end up in a circle that always brings you back to the same sad home of self-loathing. From within this circle, where you couldn't have done otherwise, you're not really confessing at all, you're merely describing.

This is why Team Smallness tends to focus on the sinner, and confession tends to always devolve into something about the self as a whole, about *who I am* instead of *what I did*. But good confession is about what I do, not who I am. It's about actions, not being.

"I'm a terrible person" is not a confession. It's a self-judgment.

"My coworkers raised $1,000 for homeless kids and I stole the money to buy a smartphone." Now that's a confession!

"I'm a sinner" is not a confession. It's a philosophy.

"I smoked crack and fondled a prostitute." Now *that's* a confession!

Good confession is empowering. Seeing a problem clearly changes the entire nature of our distress. But globalized laments keep problems woefully ambiguous. Take tarantulas, for instance. If you're like me, the thought of a tarantula on your bedroom wall above your light switch is terrifying. But even more terrifying is a tarantula *somewhere* in your bedroom. When we confess well, we give concrete form to our problems, so we can take action against them. This is partly why confession feels good, and why we all have the impulse to do it.

Consider these two prayers:

**Prayer A**

Lord, I'm a hopeless sinner. I am nothing. Desperately wicked and a pathetic stain on your great creation.

**Prayer B**

Forgive me, Father, for my recklessness with money. I blew my entire paycheck on new clothes. I get a little cash and I seem to lose my mind. I get stressed, then I buy things. And it never seems to help.

If these prayers were from two separate people, which person would be easier to help? Which person could we offer advice to? Which could we offer measurable goals to? The obvious answer is person B. There's nothing to be done for person A

Get good at confession—to others, sure, but especially to yourself and to God. Here is a three-step guide that will help get you on the right track.

1. Remove all global claims. Confessing you are a bad person is not relevant if Jesus's teaching on humility is true. All confession should be about specific acts and thoughts. It should be about problem diagnosis, not self-diagnosis.

2. State specific thoughts and behaviors. Be concrete. People have a tendency to make things abstract—especially when it comes to sin. When you confess, stay close to the ground. Confess the action you did wrong, confess what you're destroying that shouldn't be destroyed, confess the power you've abused, confess the exact lies you're telling, confess who you are hating by name, and so forth. Don't say, "Lord, forgive me for my sinning." Rather, say,

"Lord, forgive me for my pornography binge." Or, "Forgive me for my violent fantasies about the president."

3. Search for why. When we lose touch with the specifics of our sins, we can lose touch with why we are doing what we are doing. But the whys are important. The whys are the battleground of spiritual warfare. It's in the whys that Satan hides his lies. To be healed, we need to understand our whys better. We need to look for the forces that motivate our sin. What do we feel before we steal? What do we enjoy most about getting high? Why are we not content with our spouse? What precedes our spending binges?

Each sin is an opportunity for meaningful work. Dig in! Stick your mind into the soil of who you are and find the motives for why you do what you do. You may find that yelling at your kids emerges from expectations that are unreasonably high. You may discover that your hatred toward a family member has grown from a resentment of something done to you years ago. You'll find many forces in there. But finding them is like finding a pebble in your shoe. You can now work to remove it and travel with much greater comfort.

This is not to say we will solve all our problems. In this life, sin serves complicated purposes that may challenge us to the end. Nor is overcoming sin simply a matter of discovery. It isn't. Repentance is toil. But it's a good and noble toil. And without concrete and truthful confession, it's futile.

## TRAVEL TACTIC TWO: PULL YOURSELF TOGETHER

I've spent almost twenty years working with people with severe psychosis. Psychotics often become terribly fixated on specific things. One lady drank water, glass after glass, all day and all night. Gallons of it. We asked her, "Why are you drinking so much water?" She said, "Water is good for you." She's right, of course, but not that much water! We later discovered that she believed her organs were on fire, and she kept drinking water to keep the fire out.[1] Delusions make certain things seem far more important than they really are. The delusion of inequality is no different.

When we are engaged in the outside-in toil of esteemating, certain attributes seem far more important. In the hustle, we become obsessed with a handful of things—like, say, intelligence, body weight, wealth, or hair quantity. We fixate on these few things and define ourselves, and others, by them. Certain select attributes become super-important, glowing brightly before us, isolated in significance. In this way, the delusion of inequality and esteemating oversimplify our understanding of personhood. We dumb ourselves down about ourselves, and we lose touch with the rich complexity of all that we are. We allow several overheated attributes to blind us, and make us insensitive, to the complexity of self—which then leads us to make simplistic assessments of others.

People don't fit so neatly into simplistic buckets, though. Rather, we are a complicated bundle of both effective and ineffective features. But in our hustle, we zoom in on, say, ten things, leaving a hundred thousand things to blur out of focus. We are made up of many possible variables—each variable with many possible levels.

Here are a bunch that came to mind in a five-minute free-writing session. There are tons more. Look at the list. Don't fixate on any one, just appreciate the breadth:

| | | | | |
|---|---|---|---|---|
| intelligence | rhythm | complexion | size of nose | ambition |
| height | patriotism | verbal articulation | hair quantity | vocabulary |
| wealth | crassness | verbal creativity | toughness | business |
| hygiene | straightness of teeth | hair quality | patience | career desirability |
| courageousness | generousness | social influence | wittiness | generosity |
| capacity for forgiving | decisiveness | thoroughness | compassion | ability to analyze |
| body fat | youthfulness | discipline | loyalty | playfulness |
| social amiability | coordination | running speed | math skills | social intuition |
| socially distracting | personally distracted | regret | cleanliness | income |
| popularity of friends | sarcasm | memory | attention to detail | socially affirming |
| nationality | political affiliation | goal orientation | career mindedness | pitch speed |
| addiction | sound of laugh | indulgence | singing voice | marital status |
| skin color | anxiety level | skepticism tendency | investing success | honesty |
| ability to delegate | carbon footprint | criminal record | public speaking ability | disability |
| medication use | lawn care | automobile care | wardrobe quality | cleverness |
| helpfulness | emotional stability | impulsivity | tolerance for work | listening |
| assertiveness | hopefulness | empathy | studiousness | persuasiveness |
| negotiating skills | social perceptivity | ability to motivate | teachableness | ability to teach |
| family dysfunction | reading comprehension | vision | story telling ability | party facilitation |
| helpfulness | frugality | humorousness | agreeableness | weight |
| curiosity | sexual orientation | frustration tolerance | muscle tone | charitable work |
| size of feet | beard quality | perseverance | depression level | adventurousness |
| problem solving | waist size | balance | political savvy | **and on and on...** |

What we need to do is zoom out to broaden our foci. We need to build a more abundant definition of ourselves and of others. Simplistic judgments, like *good* and *bad*, are the types of extreme labels people get cognitive comfort from when they are whipsawed on the Tilt-A-Whirl of esteemating. But humility has little use for such simplistic concepts.

When we recognize the infinite possible attributes a person can have, the absurdity of calculating and judging ourselves and others based on only a few becomes clear. Seeing the overwhelming range of attributes should expose the futility and silliness of obsessing over any one attribute. It should help defuse the power of whatever attribute is causing us angst—just like owning shares of a falling stock is so much easier to handle when we own shares of forty more that are rising.

This cuts in many ways.

If I feel bad because of a weakness in one attribute, I can call to mind the infinite array of adequate attributes that I'm composed of. If I'm envious of someone else's attribute, I can remember that he, too, has an infinite array of attributes—he is probably weak in areas where I am strong. If I begin to feel haughty or arrogant because of some quality I have, the true richness of myself constrains my arrogance, as I know I have many weaknesses as well.

When we're cognizant of the entire galaxy, we don't have to get so worked up about the dimness of a single star or of a puny constellation. We don't have to get so preoccupied with whatever gifts we lack, because we possess more gifts than we probably know what to do with. We can invite criticism without shields. No matter how devastating the criticism of one thing or five things might be, we know we are so much more. We can receive the most hostile judgments with peace, because whatever judgment comes it will be understood properly, engulfed in our rich galaxy of assets.

Become aware of as many of your strengths as you can. Broaden your scope. Consider things that may even seem silly to you. For instance, I've always been incredible at driving backward. I can do it with the same ease and accuracy as driving forward. To drive backward requires the ability to invert reality. Many people struggle with this. I have no problem with it. While not particularly valuable, so far, this is a real skill, and one that would be easy to overlook.

Take a moment to write down as many strengths as you can. The quantity will impress you, I guarantee it. This is not so that we love ourselves more, exalt ourselves, or anything like that. It's simply to retrain our judgment muscles to perceive more and more of what a person is, to combat our bad habits of hyperfocus and oversimplification. Do this with your weaknesses, too—not to loathe yourself, but to recognize how bountiful you are and to deaden the sharpness of any one thing.

## TRAVEL TACTIC THREE: MANAGE MEANING

The meanings of basic things can get terribly distorted under the curse of the delusion of inequality. When we esteemate, we look at things differently, often assessing things for what they say about us, and for how they help our position in the social hierarchy. The importance of everything gets exaggerated, overdressed, and inflated, until it becomes difficult to appreciate things for what they are.

We want the things we do to be meaningful and we want our tasks to motivate us, so we seek out meaning where there may not actually be any. We love to add layers of meaning and complexity to everything. "You can tell he's a good man by his handshake," we say. But No! We can't! Handshakes don't tell us anything about a man's goodness. "If you wanna know if he loves you so, it's in his kiss," Betty Everett sang in 1963, and we can only wonder how many sorry women have been duped by soft-kissing hucksters ever since.[2]

These are silly examples, but the deviance in how we understand things can be far more serious as well. Definitions—even definitions of things that are essential for life—can get warped in the pits of the ditches and in the carnival of esteemating. Consider eating. Eating simply means:

Eat /v/ 1. To absorb, usually through the mouth, to nourish the body.

Nourish /v/ 1. providing that which fuels, enriches, or sustains.[3]

So simple.

Yet, look what's happened to us. Obesity is epidemic. Anorexia and bulimia cannonade through our schools, destroying lives. Countless souls are slaves to yo-yo diets and destructive weight-loss cults. Heart disease, a completely avoidable condition resulting from diet, punishes millions.[4] How did we mess up something so simple as eating? How have we become so confused?

We've overcomplicated eating, adding layer upon layer of extraneous meaning to it. What eating means is simple, but we can pervert this meaning in endless ways. A mom tells a boy at the dinner table, for instance, to finish all the food on his plate. He grudgingly does so, after which his family showers him with praise. "What a good boy you are!" they all exclaim. In that moment, without him even knowing it, eating has taken on a new meaning: it makes him a good boy. From that moment on, with this new layer of meaning, he will be more inclined to eat as much as he can, instead of as much as he needs. He will, therefore, be far more likely to overeat.

"I know, but it tastes good," you might say. But taste also goes beyond the basic meaning of eating. We soon expect, demand even, more and more pleasurable tastes, and food companies are happy to comply with our demands, pumping salts and sweeteners into our food—heck, even our ketchup is now loaded with sugar! A hundred years ago Americans ate, on average, seven pounds of sugar per year. Today we eat on average over a hundred pounds of it![5]

Sex is a natural, hormonal drive toward covenant bonding, which also allows for reproduction. But look how complicated we've made it! We each grow up in an avalanche of contaminated messages about sex. Some kids are told that sex is bad, or something to be ashamed of. Other kids are told that sex is the ultimate good—some are even persuaded to think that one's sex life is the utmost indicator of their effectiveness as a person. In gradual, yet powerful ways, shame and arrogance tangle into our understandings of sex, causing a thousand problems. Our understanding of sex mutates, taking on strange barnacles of meaning having to do with things like power, status, self-loathing, dominance, self-worth, and anger. It's all so self-centered. It's all so anti-relationship. It sabotages bonding and nurtures only isolation.

Food and sex are just two examples. Everything in life is susceptible to this type of definitional perversion. The world wants to warp our definitions, and esteemating and the delusion of inequality are primary contributors to this.

## DISTILL DEFINITIONS

Fighting back involves deconstructing our definitions and recovering the simple meaning of things, to deflate and undress everything until we get back to the basic core. In humility, we meditate on what things really mean, we "take captive every thought" (2 Corinthians 10:5), then guard each meaning from all the fingers and forces that want to redefine it. Eating everything on my plate does not make me a good boy because eating has little to do with my goodness or badness. Drinking beer and eating brats may taste fantastic, but it doesn't make me manlier.

Does this mean I can only eat kale? No—in fact, I'm eating Peanut M&Ms as I write this. It simply means being mindful of what eating actually is. If you have a slice of cake and a glass of wine, don't pretend you are eating (nourishing your body). Perhaps you are celebrating—which is wonderful. After all, Jesus's first miracle was to ensure there was wine at the celebration (John 2:1–11)! When you realize you're doing something other than eating, you are now in a position to treat it accordingly.

## TRAVEL TACTIC FOUR: USE YOUR DASHBOARD

If you seek God, and desire to please him, the Bible can make you dizzy. It comes at you with what seems like two antithetical messages, both equally imperative for the earnest disciple. From one side, the Bible hits you with harsh, unbending expectations. It demands obedience, with Jesus even telling his disciples to be as perfect as God (Matthew 5:48)! Then Jesus goes and hardens the Old Testament law, telling his followers that not only is adultery wrong, but merely lusting is just as deplorable (Matthew 5:28), and anger can be as disobedient as murder (Matthew 5:21–22).

While all this is coming at you, the Bible hits you with softness and tolerance. Jesus tells Peter to forgive others endlessly (Matthew 18:21–22), and since we are to love others as ourselves, it follows that we should forgive ourselves endlessly, too. He tells his followers to "be merciful, just as your Father is merciful" (Luke 6:36). James says wisdom from above is full of mercy (James 3:17), and Paul says God is the father of mercies and comfort (2 Corinthians 1:3–4).

Sometimes the Bible hits you with the harsh and the soft in the same text. James tells us we must be perfect at everything and that if we even mess up just one thing, we are no different than someone who fails at everything (James 2:8–11). This makes it sound like what we do is of utmost importance. But then in the very next paragraph he says that mercy is more important than everything (James 2:12–13). Now it seems like what we do is no big deal.

Jesus hits us with both in John 8:7–11. The crowd is about to stone an adulterous woman. Jesus steps in to argue for mercy, saying "let anyone without sin be the first to throw a stone." The crowd disperses at this, and the reader feels warm tingles. But then Jesus kills the buzz, telling the woman, "Go now and leave your life of sin."

Should I rigorously pursue obedience, or should I relax into a lifestyle of mercy?

What solved this for me was realizing both law and grace are tools God has given us to help us become the people he wants us to be. They are a means to an end. Yet we can come to view either as an end in itself, and this leads to problems.

When God's grace becomes an end, law and consequence blur out of focus. We call it *cheap grace* because it nullifies the need to obey. It deflates moral motivation. Yet, Jesus warns, "Why do you call me 'Lord, Lord,' and do not do what I say?" (Luke 6:46), and "Not everyone who says to me 'Lord, Lord,' will enter the kingdom of heaven, but only the one who does the will of my Father"

(Matthew 7:21). Grace may be sufficient for salvation—it can get us to where we want to be—but it doesn't seem sufficient to make us Christ-like disciples—it can't get us to where God wants us to be. We need expectations. We need law.

But when law becomes an end, we can easily drift into meaningless obedience and rule-keeping. Discipleship can devolve into trying to earn God's love. The importance of conduct gets amplified, and simplistic pick-your-self-up-by-your-bootstraps attitudes can emerge that suffocate compassion. People who follow this path, Jesus warns, become "whitewashed tombs . . . beautiful on the outside but on the inside . . . dead and . . . unclean" (Matthew 23:27)—basically, polished turds. The path to becoming who God wants us to be requires more than just law. We need grace.

Law and grace were never meant to be destinations, but tools we can use to get to a destination. They are a means to an end.

The kingdom of God is not about being good boys and good girls. It's about being compatible with eternal life. God doesn't want you to stop being greedy because bad boys and bad girls are greedy. He wants you to stop being greedy because greed simply doesn't work in an eternal community. God doesn't want you to stop lusting because bad boys and bad girls lust. He wants you to stop because lust doesn't work in eternal relationships.

God is calling us into advanced citizenship. This requires spiritual sophistication. We need both law and grace. Harsh, unbending law keeps us oriented to how our spiritual engine is supposed to function. Soft, lenient grace allows us to fail and start over on the complicated path to making our engine hum the way it's supposed to.

Think of a dashboard on your spiritual vessel. When we sin, a dashboard light blinks on. Something is wrong with our spiritual engine. When the light goes on, God doesn't want you to stare at the light, he wants you to look under the hood. The light itself is not as important as the problem that triggers it. God doesn't care so much that our dashboard lights are on or off. He cares that our engine is functioning properly. Viewing sin as a dashboard light like this allows us to view our sin in a way that takes obedience seriously while also remaining gentle and merciful to ourselves. We don't have to get mesmerized by the dashboard light itself, like those bent on law. Nor do we neglect the light, assuming the mechanic will fix it for us, like those bent on grace.

When you understand law and grace as means to an end, sinning—having the dashboard light come on—indicates where you are in your spiritual formation. It's a prompt that something deeper is unredeemed. It requires confession and repentance, but not self-loathing. Satan wants you to get fixated on the dashboard light and to beat yourself up. But we can be merciful to ourselves and, in peace, continue to explore the gears and pistons of our mighty spiritual machine.

## TRAVEL TACTIC FIVE: SET YOURSELF APART

People annoy me. Not everyone, but more than you might think. Sorry, but it's true. They walk too slow, talk funny, think goofy things, and so forth. They distract me and get in my way. Yet, Jesus tells me to consider them brothers and sisters (Matthew 23:8). Even worse, Paul claims I am profoundly unified—one body—with these folks (1 Corinthians 12:13). It's a problem for me. I'm the guy who'd rather take the stairs alone than ride the elevator with others. And yet, the good news of my Lord is that I am bound up intimately with them all. I try to run away from these bozos, and God is telling me to run toward them. Oh, terrible condition of mine!

God expects me to love the obnoxious, the burdensome, the smelly, the dumb, the mean, the angry, the political, the pitiful, the deplorable, the crass, the intrusive, the greedy, the racist, the violent, the pretentious, and the anyone-else-I-would-normally-avoid. That's my puzzle to solve. I can talk about unity and brotherhood and the body of Christ all day long with ease! Living all of it out, though, is a great deal trickier.

One day, I was sitting on the couch eating Peanut M&Ms and watching old *Seinfeld* reruns. Kramer, Jerry's eccentric neighbor, burst into Jerry's apartment, throwing the door open and sliding in. I couldn't take my eyes off him as he moved spastically about the kitchen while simultaneously giving a euphoric soliloquy about some crazy idea. He yanked the refrigerator door open, grabbed a carton of Jerry's milk, drank straight from the carton, put the milk back, then left Jerry's apartment in the same senseless way he entered. The show cut to commercial, and I was smiling at his antics.

Then I struck upon a curious thought. I imagined having Kramer as my own neighbor. He'd pop in unannounced through my front door, without knocking. I would be, most likely, deep in some intricate and fragile thought, maybe constructing an important article or an upcoming sermon. He'd shatter my entire thought structure with his enthusiastic ramblings of some dumb idea for a business that would never work. Then he'd go to my fridge and put his lips all over my carton of chocolate almond milk before leaving without saying goodbye.

Having Kramer in my life as a real person, I realized, would be toilsome. Yet, he made me so happy when I watched him on the show. He would make my real life a burden, but he makes a show irresistible. This anti-thetical experience of fiction-Kramer, whom I adored, and real-Kramer, whom I abhorred, intrigued me. How could I enjoy someone on television I would loathe in real life? The answer has to do with separation. Kramer, on the show, performed behind the impenetrable barrier of a television screen. My butt sat comfortably across an unsurpassable divide, immune to anything he could say or do. This buffer allowed me to enjoy someone who might normally bother me.

Then I struck upon another, more exciting thought. Humility buffers me in much the same way. As I grow in the security of humility, those around me become increasingly disarmed—much like Kramer on television. True, real people can hurt me. That is, they can cause me pain. But nobody can damage me, not in the core of my essence, not in that deep place where God embraces me in his love. Unsurpassable worth means that nobody can demote me, so it doesn't matter what people say or do to me. It doesn't matter who I dwell with. Of course, some-times people are up to no good, they engage in dangerous and sinful behavior, so I still need boundaries. But when they are not misbehaving, and when I'm in a safe place, I don't have to hide from anyone.

There's a way of viewing life and everyday interactions like a sitcom. Try this for yourself. Within the safe, pro-tective bubble of humility, where you surge with security, other people live, breathe, speak, and move behind the glass of your show. Your neighbor, your mailman, your coworker, and even me, the author of this book, are all simply characters in your sitcom. We're all bumbling along in a process that will eventually make us Christ-like masterpieces, and we will each one day be a tremendous joy to be around. But for now, in our clumsy stages of transformation, we are not always so amiable. But you are invulnerable to even our most odious deportments. Consider all of us characters that enrich your unfolding plot, your award-winning story.

In humility, you no longer have to ask what it says about you that you associate with such-and-such a person. Instead, you can wonder how that person might make your story more interesting. You can watch them in anticipation of what they are going to do next *in your story*, not in fear of what they might say or do to *you personally*.

## SET YOURSELF APART, BUT NOT TOO FAR

I know, it's strange to pursue connection by focusing on detachment, but there's good reason for it. For one thing, it works. It's worked for me, and it's worked for many of my students. Yes, connection requires, by definition, attachment. But it also requires a level of detachment.

Think of a surgeon. For many, including me, the mere sight of blood or broken bones triggers nausea, and the mere potential of a needle poke pesters us with anxiety. Yet the surgeon takes the blade and pushes it into our skin, tears open our flesh and muscle, sticks their fingers into the bloody goo of our innermost parts, then feels all around our slimy, throbbing organs. Effective surgeons must maintain maximum hypervigilance despite the repulsive nature of what they attend to. They must overcome a litany of urges, to look away, to close their eyes, to jerk back their hand, or to leave the gory scene entirely. A good surgeon must learn to dissociate from the gore.

I once worked with a patient who grabbed a handful of Monopoly game pieces and swallowed them. The nurse asked my coworkers and me to locate the game pieces on an x-ray of the patient's stomach. Several of us stood around the illuminated image, pointing to various spots, calling out, "there's the car" and "I think this is a hotel" and "here's the shoe." We played this strange game of Where's Waldo every day for at least a week, counting whatever remaining pieces had not yet been pooped out. Eventually there was only one piece left that refused to pass: the horse.

The decision was made to have the horse surgically removed, and I was asked to escort the patient to the operating room. As the nurses prepared the patient, I struck up a conversation with the surgeon. I asked her how she handles the gore. She confessed that, early on, she relied heavily on her imagination. She said she'd pretend her own body was a machine, operated by remote control. She noted that a person cringes and retreats from gore, but a machine doesn't. In the same way, she imagined her eyes as cameras sending her images from far away. These acts of imagination put her in a state of mind that kept her effectively distant from the triggers, yet still allowed her to be effectively present to perform the surgery. At some point, she said, she no longer needed to enter into this make-believe. The dissociated presence became natural to her.

The tactic I am prescribing is very much like this.

Humbling yourself has much to do with setting yourself apart in the right way and at the right distance.

## BECOME THE DIRECTOR OF YOUR SITCOM

Viewing life as a show like this can orient your thinking in a helpful way. Instead of focusing on everything happening to you, try focusing on the story of what's happening. Focusing on story, instead of self, keeps you from taking things too personally by helping you see everything that happens in a greater context. This, in turn, dulls the impact of whatever happens.

When you designate a bothersome person as simply a character in your story, you set a boundary, a barrier between you and them, that will often deaden your natural impulse to detach from them. You don't have to take what they do personally. They're just playing a role. Sometimes what people say and do to you, though they make for terrible moments in your life, can become pivotal scenes in your story. In this way, your suffering can be redeemed, and your anger or hatred for a person can be transformed into something like appreciation. It also keeps you future-oriented. Good or bad, failure or success, we don't have to ask *what does this say about me?* We can ask *what is my character going to do next?*

God empowers you to be the director of your show. In humility, you can float through each moment with peace and patience, letting each relationship be what it is, and letting each person be who they are. You don't have to control others or demand they change. Sure, set boundaries with people, build them up, and challenge them—after all, you're a character in your story, too. But you don't have to manage them or let them manage you.

In humility, you can observe people and be with them without judgment or expectation. You can accept and appreciate them for where they are at. Help them when you can, let them be who they are when you cannot.

In humility we don't have to filter, control, or avoid people who are different from us. We don't have to be so picky about who we fellowship with. No doubt, if you surround yourself with like-minded people and go to churches with congregations full of people who are just like you, this will make for an easy, enjoyable life. But it makes for a humdrum, tedious, boring show. So, go out there and be with people! In humility, you can dwell with a wide, fantastic variety of wonderfully strange characters all over God's creation. This makes for a far more interesting show—a show you can't take your eyes off.

# APPENDIX: THE WORST OF SINNERS AND FOOT WASHING

Some verses seem curiously contrary to Jesus's teaching on equality. At times, both Jesus and Paul seem to encourage self-demotion, not equality. Here are two examples.

## JESUS WASHES THE DISCIPLES' FEET

The argument could be made that if Jesus lowers himself to wash the feet of others (John 13:1–17), and he calls his disciples to do the same, it follows that being humble has much to do with lowering the self as much as possible.

Although it's a compelling way to read the text, I think it's a flawed interpretation. In fact, reading the text in this spirit simply affirms the broken social construct Jesus was actually opposing: that washing feet says something about your worth. Jesus wasn't lowering himself to a despicable task to put on a show of despicability. He was shattering the notion that such silly tasks actually mean something about our value to begin with. He was confronting the idea that being a servant meant you were somehow worth less than those you are serving.

Jesus wasn't teaching us to condescend and serve one another, he was teaching us that we should not regard service as condescension to begin with. Service isn't what unimportant people do for important people, it's what equals do for each other.

## CONSIDER YOURSELF THE "WORST OF SINNERS," AND "IN HUMILITY REGARD OTHERS AS BETTER THAN YOURSELVES"

Paul challenges us to regard others as better than ourselves, even to the extent that we ought to view ourselves as the "worst of sinners" (1 Timothy 1:15, author's paraphrase). This seems a blatant call to consider ourselves as less than others. But I don't think this is the case. What Paul is offering here is not a literal evaluation of the self but rather a sort of lifestyle tactic or a discipleship strategy.

This may sound like a cop-out, but hear me out. We can apply a simple test to any command like this to show whether it should be taken literally or not. For instance, in Matthew 7:3–5, Jesus tells his listeners to stop focusing on the speck of dust in their neighbor's eye when they themselves have a plank of wood in their own eye. Ask the question: Can a literal interpretation of this verse be applied to everyone? I would say, in this case, it cannot. It's impossible for everyone's sin to be bigger than everyone else's. Jesus doesn't tell his listeners to believe impossible things. He is, rather, suggesting a tactic to help us stay focused on what should be our priority: our own sin.

Paul is simply reiterating Jesus's tactic. When we each think of ourselves as the worst sinner, it helps us to avoid the powerful urge to judge the sins of others. We can't all be the worst of sinners just as we can't all have sins (planks) bigger than everyone else's (specks). These commands are tactical. They're meant to help us attain a spiritual state that is not natural to us.

# ENDNOTES

## ACKNOWLEDGMENTS

1. He didn't really threaten to beat me up. But he did motivate me to start writing.

## CHAPTER 1: A TALE OF TWO DITCHES

1. No doubt, there can be advantages to growing up with less parental presence. When you don't have the preconditioning of parents, it's easier to look at things more objectively and dispassionately. This is a powerful cognitive liberty. It's why I've often said it is better to have no parents than to have lousy parents.

2. The diagnosis made me think I was dumb, or slow. Looking back at it now, especially after having worked with hundreds of kids in situations similar to my own, I realize that I wasn't necessarily slow. Rather, I was obliged to process *more*. I was compensating for an absence of parental programming.

3. Military kids, who are often required to change schools frequently, have told me they've experienced this same social capriciousness.

4. Sigmund Freud thought we each have sexual desires toward a parent and, simultaneously, we each have latent

homicidal urges toward the competing parent. He believed this deep perversion and violence was a biological reality that was natural to us and mostly inescapable. This hideousness seeps out into all areas of our lives. Psychoanalysis has much to do with exploring these natural drives and selfish impulses. Progress involves giving ample attention (psychoanalysis can go on for decades) to this more real, depraved self, lurking beneath the less real, socially appropriate self we each fashion for society. Pantheism also champions a deprecated view of self. The philosophic core of pantheism is that there is only spirit; there is no matter. Ultimate salvation for Buddhism (nirvana) and Hinduism (moksha) involves a complete liberation from the lie of self.

5. Martin Luther, *The Bondage of the Will*, trans. James I. Packer and O. R. Johnston (Old Tappan, NJ: Revell, 1957), 241.

6. John Calvin, *The Institutes of Christian Religion*, ed. Tony Lane and Hilary Osborne (Grand Rapids: Baker, 1987), 1.1.3.

7. C. J. Mahaney, *Humility: True Greatness* (Sisters, OR: Multnomah, 2005), 31.

8. Some will say that we can accomplish things on our own, just not with a pure heart. Whatever we accomplish will be born out of some selfish ambition.

9. Dallas Willard, *The Divine Conspiracy: Rediscovering Our Hidden Life in God* (San Francisco: HarperSanFrancisco, 1998), 102.

10. Terry D. Cooper, *Sin, Pride, and Self-Acceptance: The Problem of Identity in Theology and Psychology* (Downers Grove, IL: InterVarsity, 2003), 26.

11. Roy F. Baumeister, Jennifer D. Campbell, Joachim I. Krueger, and Kathleen D. Vohs, "Does High Self-Esteem

Cause Better Performance, Interpersonal Success, Happiness, or Healthier Lifestyles?" *Psychological Science in the Public Interest* 4, no. 1 (2003): 3.

12. Baumeister et al., "Does High Self-Esteem Cause Better Performance," 1.

13. Barbara Ehrenreich, *Bright-Sided: How the Relentless Promotion of Positive Thinking Has Undermined America* (New York: Metropolitan Books, 2009), 52.

14. Mr. Dyer made this comment in many of his presentations. See "Wayne Dyer—When You Change the Way You Look at Things," YouTube video, 3:36, uploaded by "hamohd70," April 19, 2008, https://tinyurl.com/y9xnrv6r.

15. Joel Osteen, *Become a Better You: 7 Keys to Improving Your Life Every Day* (New York: Howard Books, 2017).

## CHAPTER 2: THE ROAD TO SECURITY

1. Wayne A. Mack and Joshua Mack, *Humility: The Forgotten Virtue* (Phillipsburg, NJ: P&R Publications, 2005), 25–26.

2. C. Peter Wagner, *Humility* (Ventura, CA: Regal, 2002), 6.

3. Mack and Mack, *Humility*, 33.

4. Andrew Murray, *Humility* (Springdale, PA: Whitaker, 1982), 59.

5. Stuart Scott, *From Pride to Humility: A Biblical Perspective* (Bemidji, MN: Focus, 2002), 12. Scott makes it clear that we are no worse than anyone else for, we are *all* desperately wicked. He qualifies our depravity, specifying that we are worthless as compared to God.

6. Evelyn Underhill, *The Cloud of Unknowing* (Stilwell, KS: Neeland, 2011), 45.

7. Friedrich Wilhelm Nietzsche, *Basic Writings of Nietzsche*, trans. William August Haussmann (Boston: Digireads, 2012).

8. My friend Ben Damman came up with this word. He's very clever and a darn good programmer.

9. Greg Boyd, "What Is God's Glory?" March 16th, 2017, episode 126 of *Apologies and Explanations*, produced by Reknew.org, podcast, 8:15.

10. Norvin Richards, *Humility* (Philadelphia: Temple University Press, 1992), 169.

11. The clause "and sisters" added by the author throughout.

12. Donald L. Nathanson, *Shame and Pride: Affect, Sex, and the Birth of the Self* (New York: Norton, 1992), 86. See also James Kellenberger, "Humility," *American Philosophical Quarterly* 47, no. 4 (2010): 329.

13. J. Mark Beach, "God's Lion or His Humble Servant? Preaching and Humility: 'Serving the Lord with All Humility' (Acts 20:19)," *Mid-America Journal of Theology* 22 (2011): 184.

14. Kellenberger, "Humility," 329.

15. See John Calvin's Commentary on the Psalms, 9:1–3.

16. David K. Clark, "Philosophical Reflections on Self-Worth and Self-Love," *Journal of Psychology and Theology* 13, no.1 (1985): 5.

17. So much so that Mark tells us he had to learn right and wrong (Luke 2:52).

18. Dallas Willard, *The Divine Conspiracy: Rediscovering Our Hidden Life in God* (San Francisco: HarperSanFrancisco, 1998), 222.

19. June Price Tangney and Ronda L. Dearing, *Shame and Guilt* (New York: Guilford, 2004), 20.

20. Tangney and Dearing, *Shame and Guilt*, 20.

21. This brilliant analogy was provided by my wife. For the record, her father was sweet and loving, and you were always welcome to spill his beer.

22. Tangney and Dearing, *Shame and Guilt*, 81–85.

23. Michael Lewis, *The Big Short: Inside the Doomsday Machine* (New York: W. W. Norton, 2011).

24. Lewis, *The Big Short*, 86.

25. Lewis, *The Big Short*, 88.

26. Lewis, *The Big Short*, 87.

27. Valerie Tiberius and John D. Walker, "Arrogance," *American Philosophical Quarterly* 35, no. 4 (1998): 380.

28. Tiberius and Walker, "Arrogance," 384.

29. Gregory A. Boyd, *Benefit of the Doubt: Breaking the Idol of Certainty* (Grand Rapids: Baker, 2013), 240.

30. Wayne A. Mack and Joshua Mack, *Humility: The Forgotten Virtue* (Phillipsburg, NJ: P&R Publications, 2005), 26.

31. Terry D. Cooper, *Sin, Pride, and Self-Acceptance: The Problem of Identity in Theology and Psychology* (Downers Grove, IL: InterVarsity, 2003), 106.

32. Barbara Ehrenreich, *Bright-Sided: How the Relentless Promotion of Positive Thinking Has Undermined America* (New York: Metropolitan Books, 2009), 74–75.

33. Ehrenreich, *Bright-Sided*, 80.

34. George Beecher, for instance, circa 1843.

35. Now we would diagnose such a person with various anxiety and depressive disorders.

36. See Rukmini Callimachi, "A Dream Ended on a Mountain Road: The Cyclists and the ISIS Militants," *New York Times*, August 7, 2018, https://tinyurl.com/yd8wo5m3; Rukmini Callimachi and Andrew E. Kramer, "Video Purports to Show Tajikistan Attackers Pledging

Allegiance to ISIS," *New York Times*, July 31, 2018, https://tinyurl.com/ybkubua3.

37. Callimachi, "A Dream Ended on a Mountain Road," https://tinyurl.com/yd8wo5m3.

38. Jay Austin, @simplycycling, Instagram, https://www.instagram.com/simplycycling/.

## CHAPTER 3: THE ROAD TO EQUALITY

1. Notice, too, that Jesus doesn't say: "You are all children." Children are coddled by their parents. Nor does he say, "You are all citizens." Citizens are competitive and cutthroat, and they show very little care for one another. Jesus says, "You are all siblings." Even in most dysfunctional families, siblings have a unique bond. They certainly don't coddle one another, and there is always competition. Yet, it's not the heartless competition of society. Siblings are competitive yet caring. They challenge one another and value one another.

2. Gregory A. Boyd, *The Crucifixion of the Warrior God: Interpreting the Old Testament's Violent Portraits of God in Light of the Cross* (Minneapolis: Fortress Press, 2017).

3. In modern times we tend to view death in more graded terms (for instance, a person could be merely brain dead). In Paul's day that was not the case.

4. I know, right!?! Terrible!

5. Martin E. P. Seligman and Steven F. Maier, "Failure to Escape Traumatic Shock," *Journal of Experimental Psychology* 74 (1967): 1–9.

6. Reinhard Feldmeier and Brian McNeil, *Power, Service, Humility: A New Testament Ethic* (Waco, TX: Baylor University Press, 2014), 64.

7. Jürgen Moltmann, "Control Is Good—Trust Is Better:

Freedom and Security in a 'Free World,'" *Theology Today* 62, no. 4 (2006): 467.

8. Not sure where this originates. Dozens on social media have used it as if it was their own.

9. See "Blame the Self-Esteem Movement for Rise of Trump | Real Time with Bill Maher (HBO)," YouTube video, 6:42, uploaded by "Real Time with Bill Maher," March 18, 2016, https://tinyurl.com/gtpvd56.

10. William R. Drennan, *Prairie House: Frank Lloyd Wright and the Taliesin Murders* (Madison: University of Wisconsin Press, 2008), 71.

11. See David G. Myers, "The Psychology of Humility," in *God, Science, and Humility: Ten Scientists Consider Humility Theology*, ed. Robert L. Herrmann (Philadelphia: Templeton Foundation Press, 2000), 153–75.

12. "The Key to Reconciliation," September 28, 2003, in *The Meeting House Teaching Series*, sermon, 41:05, https://tinyurl.com/y9zlzz25.

13. "The Key to Reconciliation," https://tinyurl.com/y9zlzz25.

14. Plus, retributive justice is founded on the ideal of everyone "getting what they deserve." But a culprit getting what they deserve for an offense is often not just either, since they started under conditions that they neither chose nor deserved.

## CHAPTER 4: TRAVELING ON A DANGEROUS ROAD: ESTEEMATING

1. Andrew Murray (*Humility: The Beauty of Holiness* [Abbotsford, WI: Aneko, 2016], 10) goes a step further, saying pride is the "root of every sin and evil." Saint Chrysostom echoes this, claiming that "pride is the

mother of all evils" (quoted in Wayne A. Mack and Joshua Mack, *Humility: The Forgotten Virtue* [Phillipsburg, NJ: P&R Publications, 2005], 60–61).

2. Richard Winter, *Perfecting Ourselves to Death: The Pursuit of Excellence and the Perils of Perfectionism* (Downers Grove, IL: InterVarsity, 2005), 126.

3. Can you see how frustrating debates between the Ditch of Smallness and the Ditch of Bigness can be? They can each read the same biblical texts and draw totally different conclusions. They both walk away from the Bible feeling totally validated by it. One sees pride as the problem, the other sees shame as the problem. Yet so often the Bible simply records actions without specifying shame or pride, and either shame or pride can be read into the text.

4. Terry D. Cooper, *Sin, Pride, and Self-Acceptance: The Problem of Identity in Theology and Psychology* (Downers Grove, IL: InterVarsity, 2003), 16.

5. Albert Camus, *The Myth of Sisyphus: And Other Essays*, trans. Justin O'Brien (New York: Vintage Books, 1959), 7.

6. Michael K. Farr, *The Arrogance Cycle: Think You Can't Lose, Think Again; What Every Investor Needs to Know to Protect Their Assets from the Next Big Bubble* (Guilford, CT: Lyons Press, 2011), 1.

7. Winter, *Perfecting Ourselves to Death*, 61.

8. Dallas Willard, *The Divine Conspiracy: Rediscovering Our Hidden Life in God* (San Francisco: HarperSanFrancisco, 1998), 181.

9. Dusya Vera and Antonio Rodriguez-Lopez, "Humility as a Source of Competitive Advantage," *Organizational Dynamics* 33, no. 4 (2004): 395.

10. F. LeRon Shults and Steven J. Sandage, *The Faces of Forgiveness: Searching for Wholeness and Salvation* (Grand Rapids: Baker Academic, 2003), 60.

11. Everett L. Worthington, *Humility: The Quiet Virtue* (Philadelphia: Templeton Foundation Press, 2007).

12. David G. Myers, "The Psychology of Humility," in *God, Science, and Humility: Ten Scientists Consider Humility Theology*, ed. Robert L. Herrmann (Philadelphia: Templeton Foundation Press, 2000), 174.

13. Shults and Sandage, *The Faces of Forgiveness*, 60.

## CHAPTER 5: THE ROAD TO TRANSFORMATION

1. Timothy Keller, "The Advent of Humility," *Christianity Today*, December 2008, 53.

2. Keller, "Advent of Humility," 53.

3. Keller, "Advent of Humility," 53.

4. John Piper, "Lewis and Edwards on the Layers of Self-Admiration," *Desiring God* (blog), August 18, 2009, https://tinyurl.com/ycyl9dap.

5. C. J. Mahaney, *Humility: True Greatness* (Sisters, OR: Multnomah, 2005), 84–85.

## CHAPTER 6: THE ROAD TO EMPOWERMENT

1. John P. Dickson, *Humilitas: A Lost Key to Life, Love, and Leadership* (Grand Rapids: Zondervan, 2011), 25.

2. C. Peter Wagner, *Humility* (Ventura, CA: Regal, 2002), 8.

3. Thomas Jones and Michael Fontenot, *The Prideful Soul's Guide to Humility* (Billerica, MA: Discipleship Publications International, 2003), 17.

4. Andrew Murray, *Humility* (Springdale, PA: Whitaker, 1982), 3.

5. John Piper, Justin Taylor, and Paul Kjoss Helseth, *Beyond the Bounds: Open Theism and the Undermin-*

*ing of Biblical Christianity* (Wheaton, IL: Crossway, 2003), 88.

6. "Trust God" is unanimously prescribed but never defined. It ends up being a catch-all prescription. "How do I stop being proud?" Answer: "Trust God." "What does this mean?" "It means to stop being proud."

7. "If any of you lacks wisdom, you should ask God, who gives generously to all without finding fault, and it will be given to you" (James 1:5), and, "These are the ones I look on with favor: those who are humble" (Isaiah 66:2).

8. Jones and Fontenot, *Prideful Soul's Guide*, 62.

9. Jones and Fontenot, *Prideful Soul's Guide*, 59.

10. Barbara Ehrenreich, *Bright-Sided: How the Relentless Promotion of Positive Thinking Has Undermined America* (New York: Metropolitan Books, 2009), 63.

11. Ehrenreich, *Bright-Sided*, 49–51; Sue Morter, "There Is Only One of Us Here," DrSueMorter.com, September 26, 2013, https://tinyurl.com/y8rrurbp.

12. Miroslav Volf, *Exclusion and Embrace: A Theological Exploration of Identity, Otherness, and Reconciliation* (Nashville: Abingdon, 1996), 122.

## CHAPTER 7: THE ROAD TO CONFIDENCE

1. Laurent Bègue, Brad J. Bushman, Oulmann Zerhouni, Baptiste Subra, and Medhi Ourabah, "'Beauty Is in the Eye of the Beer Holder': People Who Think They Are Drunk Also Think They Are Attractive," *British Journal of Psychology* 104, no. 2 (2013): 225–34.

2. Janet Polivy and C. Peter Herman, "If at First You Don't Succeed: False Hope of Self-Change," *American Psychologist* 57, no. 9 (2002): 683.

3. Lyn Y. Abramson, Martin E. P. Seligman, and John

D. Teasdale, "Learned Helplessness in Humans: Critique and Reformulation," *Journal of Abnormal Psychology* 87, no. 1 (1978): 61.

4. Vivien J. Lewis, Alan J. Blair, and David A. Booth, "Outcome of Group Therapy for Body-Image Emotionality and Weight-Control Self-Efficacy," *Behavioural Psychotherapy* 20, no. 2 (1992): 155–66.

5. Mark B. Sobell, Linda C. Sobell, and Douglas R. Gavin. "Portraying Alcohol Treatment Outcomes: Different Yardsticks of Success," *Behavior Therapy* 26, no. 4 (1995): 643–69.

6. In fact, ironically, it is even arrogant in at least two ways. First, how do you know your no-hitter was a blessing from God? Do you have special access to God? Second, it suggests you are being used in some special way by God. Like you are some favored child. God has chosen you for this special mission, a holy task. You are not like all those others whom God has not given this blessing.

7. Tomas Chamorro-Premuzic, *Confidence: Overcoming Low Self-esteem, Insecurity, and Self-Doubt* (New York: Hudson Street, 2013), 40.

8. Polivy and Herman, "If at First You Don't Succeed," 677.

9. Polivy and Herman, "If at First You Don't Succeed," 685.

10. Patricia Perry, "Concept Analysis: Confidence/Self-Confidence," *Nursing Forum* 46, no. 4 (2011): 222.

## CHAPTER 8: THE ROAD TO SOCIAL VITALITY

1. So they are each, in this way, quantitative and self-oriented loves.

2. Bruxy Cavey, "Let Love Lead," June 23, 2013, Wood-

land Hills Church, sermon, 40:55, https://tinyurl.com/ya27gwea.

3. Gregory A. Boyd, *Repenting of Religion: Turning from Judgment to the Love of God* (Grand Rapids: Baker, 2004), 44.

4. Larry Crabb, *Connecting: Healing for Ourselves and Our Relationships; A Radical New Vision* (Nashville: Word Pub, 1997), xiv.

5. Crabb, *Connecting*, xviii.

6. Crabb, *Connecting*, 38.

7. "A mocker does not respond to rebukes" (Proverbs 13:1).

8. Transforming into agape lovers, into kingdom kids, also requires some self-focus (just as confidence did). Self-focus is a means to an end—namely, the means to become more effective at living out other-centered, agape love. Too much self-focus sabotages agape in that the other is neglected and our love atrophies. Too little self-focus sabotages agape in that the self is neglected and our ability to love atrophies.

9. Cavey, "Let Love Lead," https://tinyurl.com/ya27gwea.

10. Crabb, *Connecting*, 32.

11. C. S. Lewis, *Letters to an American Lady*, ed. Clyde S. Kilby (Grand Rapids: Eerdmans, 1996), 75–76.

12. Cited in Boyd, *Repenting of Religion*, 58.

## CHAPTER 9: A HUMBLE TRAVELER

1. What she was actually doing was flushing her medications out of her body, keeping her in her delusional state.

2. Betty Everett, "Shoop Shoop Song (It's in His Kiss)," written by Rudy Clark, BMG Rights Management, 1964.

3. These definitions are my own syntheses from a variety of dictionaries.

4. See Michael Greger and Gene Stone, *How Not to Die: Discover the Foods Scientifically Proven to Prevent and Reverse Disease* (London: Pan Books, 2018).

5. Michael Greger, "Does Diet Soda Increase Stroke Risk as Much as Regular Soda?," NutritionFacts.org, video, 7:20, https://tinyurl.com/ybdfq9lg.